MW01156756

The Inn at Little Washington Cookbook

Patrick O'Connell

The Inn at Little Washington Cookbook
A Consuming Passion

Patrick O'Connell
Photographs by Tim Turner

RANDOM HOUSE   NEW YORK

ISBN: 0-679-44736-9

Library of Congress Cataloguing-in-Publication information is available.

Random House website address: http://www.randomhouse.com/

Printed in the United States of America on acid-free paper

98765432

First Edition

ACKNOWLEDGMENTS

This book evolved with the help and inspiration of many individuals to whom I am indebted: First, the former editorial director of Random House, Jason Epstein, whose passion for cooking provided the necessary catalyst to get the project under way. Working with photographer Tim Turner was a joyous experience; his artistry contributed another dimension to my work. The supplementary photographs by Kay Chernush and Eric Rasmussen brilliantly capture the singular beauty of the surrounding countryside. The enthusiasm of the book's designers, Adam Kallish, Elizabeth Nelson, and Pat Noonan-Hastings of Trope: Communication by Design, was a godsend. Bob Barnett, my attorney, managed to make all the legal negotiations stress-free. Laura Patton, my assistant, in addition to typing the manuscript, managed to keep the project on track. My kitchen staff helped compose, reduce, and test some of the recipes and had to put up with additional intensity from me as the book's deadline approached. Ellen Brown helped with the editing of the final few recipes.

Special thanks are extended to our local farmers and purveyors for their co-operation in working with us on this project; for allowing photographers to wander through their orchards, barns, and chicken houses; and for lending us props for our photo shoots. We also appreciate their commitment to providing us with the superlative raw ingredients that are the essence of great cooking. We are most grateful to Goat Hill Farm, Jordan River Farm, Moore's Orchard, Henry Hudson, Elizabeth Pierson, Tom Calhoun of Calhoun's Ham House, and the Sperryville Antique Center for being such good neighbors.

I thank Bernard Loiseau, a friend and one of France's most celebrated chefs, for donating a recipe as a souvenir of our cooking together on his first trip to America.

A special acknowledgment to my partner, Reinhardt Lynch, whose support and encouragement helped make this book possible.

CONTENTS

STOCKS, SAUCES, AND SUNDRY

INTRODUCTION

Probably the best and the worst thing that ever happened to me was that I got a job in a restaurant at the impressionable age of fifteen.

The addiction was immediate. Once I discovered the pace and intensity of this delicious business, I was hooked. I found restaurant people to be fascinating characters. Whoever was writing this script had an outrageous sense of humor, and I wanted a part in the production.

I was supposed to have become an actor but soon found the living theater of the restaurant world more compelling than the stage and discovered that working with food gave me a much-needed grounding and connection with the real world, which contributed to my remaining somewhat sane. Running a restaurant allows me to be the producer, director, set designer, and lead player in a wonderfully fractured nightly performance in which the world of complete illusion in the dining room is brilliantly juxtaposed with the blood-and-guts reality of the kitchen. The fact that no scene can ever be captured or exactly replicated adds a certain spice to the intensity of the moment.

This book is a distillation of my thirty years in the kitchen. Many of the recipes I have included are like old friends who have been brought from distant places for a culinary version of *This Is Your Life.* Each one has a story to tell and relates to the others. Collectively, they define a style and taste that are uniquely American, though full of influences from other countries.

This is not a typical chef's cookbook of esoteric, egomaniacal, and impossibly complicated formulas that only a wizard with a staff of eighty would attempt to produce. The recipes assembled here make up a practiced, finely honed repertoire of elegantly simple and straightforward dishes that are continually evolving. Everyday ingredients are elevated to new heights through surprising combinations and seductive presentations.

As a self-taught chef, I have learned my most valuable lessons through making mistakes. I hope this book will keep you from making similar ones. You should be encouraged to know that I taught myself to cook by reading cookbooks and through years of trial and error. I was recently quoted in the book *Becoming a Chef* as saying that cooking "can't be taught, it has to be caught"—rather like a fever, which then takes on a momentum of its own. This book is intended to help you catch it—to become consumed with the passion.

In addition to some of my favorite recipes, I want to share some of the less tangible secrets of creating a memorable event centered around a meal. Great food is simply one component of a magical dining experience.

In planning a menu, I always aim for an element of novelty. A guest expects the food to be delicious and perfectly executed but also craves the unexpected surprise—something to remember and talk about. Often it's the tiniest details that leave the most indelible memories. They represent the thoughtfulness that goes into making an occasion special and are often personal touches that cost little or nothing.

For example, hand-writing individual menus on interesting little cards that include the date lets the guests know what they're eating and gives them an inexpensive souvenir of your party. Enhancing the moment by emphasizing the season in both your choice of food and its presentation strengthens the memory-making potential of a dinner party. Try to make each meal a celebration of the moment: look for ingredients that symbolize the time of year and try to do something out of the ordinary with them.

My suggestion for the home cook has always been to build confidence and a repertoire by mastering one well-conceived three-course meal, re-creating the same three dishes over and over, perhaps one night a week for six or eight weeks, until you've made every mistake possible and learned something from each one. By then, your menu will feel like a part of you, and you'll be amazed at how quickly you can accomplish the preparation. At that point, you'll be ready to invite guests, who more than likely will be astonished at what an accomplished cook you are, even though secretly you may not be able to cook anything but those three dishes. You'll then have the confidence to proceed and live up to your newfound reputation as a wonderful cook.

Like a good wardrobe, many of the components in my recipes are interchangeable. I invite you to rearrange them as you like. At The Inn at Little Washington we sometimes joke about "spinning the dial" in choosing the accompaniments to the dishes on the menu. One day the tangle of tart greens may be served with the rabbit sausage and the next day with the venison. An unusual sauce may complement five or six different foods. Mixing and matching is part of the fun. I've provided suggestions for substitutions with the recipes, as well as alternative ways of using various components interchangeably. Flexibility is essential to creative cooking.

In planning a party or an event, I visualize it in advance, as if I'm watching the preview of a film. I pretend I'm the guest and walk myself through it scene by scene, from the entrance, to the table, through dessert and departure, looking for areas of potential discomfort, glitches, or rough edges. This exercise can be done in minutes and will always bring to your attention details that you forgot to take into consideration. While on your walk-through you'll probably come up with great ideas for special touches.

It's reassuring to have a little rehearsal of the meal a few days in advance to ensure that everything works and to analyze how the food makes you feel. As a result, you may decide to add or delete a course or to increase or decrease a portion size.

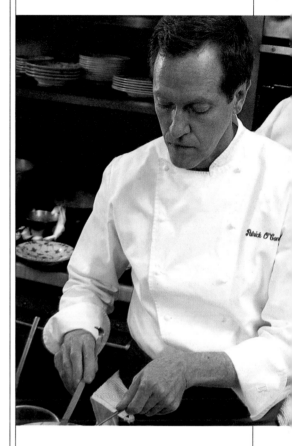

The best way to minimize stress while entertaining is to be thoroughly organized. Knowing exactly what china and serving utensils will be needed for each dish is important. If you make this a habit while cooking for yourself or preparing simple family meals, it will eventually become automatic. A blackboard in the kitchen is useful for listing your menu, garnishes, and side dishes to ensure that nothing is forgotten in the tense final moments of bringing everything together. Most of us can remember at least one occasion when we discovered that a course we'd spent hours preparing was left unserved in the kitchen.

To improve your cooking, it is essential that you receive helpful criticism. Find someone whose opinion you value and ask him or her to be brutally honest in critiquing your work. Don't rely on your guests or friends because they'll invariably tell you everything you cook is wonderful. Compare your creations with similar dishes in fine restaurants. Begin developing reference points of taste. While traveling, seek out and analyze the great dishes of the regions you're visiting and try them at home. Compare the results and keep practicing until your version is even better than the original. Each time you prepare a dish, ask yourself, "How can I make it better and do it faster next time?" Fantasize about how you would like your food to look and taste and, amazingly, in time, little by little, your fantasy will become a reality.

But be careful. All your dreams could come true, and one day you might wake up owning a restaurant.

THE STORY OF THE INN
AT LITTLE WASHINGTON

❦

For an American kid in the 1960s, joining the circus seemed more realistic than a career in the restaurant business. Only after I spent a year traveling in Europe did I begin to understand the potential for artistic fulfillment as a chef.

In France I sensed a very different attitude toward chefs. They were taken as seriously as performing artists or athletes were in the States. The admiration of great restaurants approached religious fervor. Crowds gathered to peer into pastry shop windows. A childlike wonderment and excitement seemed to surround everything having to do with food, while back home restaurants meant deep fryers, waitresses with run-over white-soled shoes, and maraschino cherries.

I returned to the United States with a new appreciation for the art of the table, but I still couldn't figure out what I wanted to be when I grew up, so I postponed the process for as long as possible and moved to the country to clear my head.

I lived on a farm, ate from my garden, and bathed in the river. In the winter, I spent a lot of time in the library of the nearest town because it had central heat. At night, I'd bring home cookbooks and keep warm by baking in the wood cookstove. This was the beginning of an uncontrollable obsession.

I cooked night and day. Friends would joke that I'd cook anything I could get my hands on—even pets weren't safe. Visitors increased as my cooking improved. Company was always welcome. I would even invite lost hikers from nearby Shenandoah National Park in for a meal. Soon enough everybody began saying, "You should open a restaurant."

Meanwhile, my friend Reinhardt Lynch, whom I'd known and worked with in Washington, D.C., visited on his way to Boston and liked country living so well he never left. Before long the two of us became partners in a catering business. O'Connell–Lynch Caterers operated out of the farmhouse kitchen, using the wood cookstove as well as an electric frying pan we bought at a yard sale for $1.59.

Our clients were members of the local gentry who were adventurous enough to try something other than their usual leaden biscuits and salty ham. One thing led to another, and soon we were catering garden weddings and formal dinners for three hundred. Local flower children living in the nearby woods—some with names like Birdwing or Running Deer—were recruited, bathed, and trucked in to the parties to serve as waiters or additional kitchen staff.

We bought all our food at the Safeway, forty miles away, brought it home to the farm, and carried it across a footbridge to the house, which was on the wrong side of the river. When the footbridge washed out once a month or so, we waded across. In the winter, the bridge was often covered with ice.

We developed a technique we called "slithering" to get the groceries across. This involved lying on your stomach, holding on to the icy bridge with your left hand, and clutching a heavy sack of groceries with your right hand while squirming across like a caterpillar to the other side. The same ordeal would begin in reverse when we had to carry the finished dishes back across the river in a parade of canapés, tarts, trees of shrimp, and domes of pâté, with the wedding cake usually bringing up the rear.

We had many memorable disasters. Once a very tiny young woman dressed as a French maid—complete with starched, frilly white apron—who was riding in the back of our van fell headfirst into an enormous container of marinated mushrooms when we hit a bump. Finally, one day in the kitchen, still exhausted from a wedding the day before, I said to Reinhardt, "Why don't we make them come to us?"

Four years later, in the urbane village of Washington, Virginia, The Inn at Little Washington opened for business during the worst blizzard of the decade. We'd managed to save $5,000 and borrow enough to build a kitchen. Our rent was $200 a month—top dollar for a defunct garage. The upstairs had been a basketball court and dance hall. The gas pumps had been removed, a porch had been added, and it was operating as a country store. We transformed the front of the building into a dining room and cooked in the back.

As you might imagine, finding help was a problem in a village of 158 souls. Knowing the lifestyle of the local counterculture all too well, we asked in our first mimeographed application form: "Do you have a bathtub?" We soon realized that the language was not specific enough when a kitchen worker tattled on a waitress. The waitress had not been untruthful—she did have a bathtub, but it was in her backyard, where somebody had dumped it along with an old school bus.

Our first waiter had no shoes except for a pair of combat boots, and he wasn't about to invest in a pair at the local Kmart because "nobody was bettin' this venture would fly." So we compromised—he let me spray-paint his boots black.

Opening night—two hours before the first guests were to arrive—I was seized by violent abdominal pains. I crawled under table eleven and squeezed the center post as hard as I could. What a rotten time to have an attack of appendicitis, I thought. I was hollering for the rescue squad when the phone rang. It was a woman we knew who also owned a restaurant, calling to wish us well on the opening. I crawled to the phone and told her what was happening, and she said: "Well, whaddaya expect? You're giving birth, aren't ya? Don't worry. This is normal. It's nerves, dahling—just nerves. The show must go on. Get back to the stove and everything will be all right." I did. And the show went on . . . and on.

The locals watched, amazed that there were that many people who would pay up to $8.95 for dinner. Opening week the roast chicken with fresh tarragon and green beans was only $4.95, but it quickly jumped to $5.95 several days later.

During the second week, we were visited anonymously by the restaurant critic of the second biggest newspaper in Washington, D.C. On his way out he asked to speak to me and said, "I never do this, but I'm going to introduce myself because I have to ask if you really want me to write about this place."

I assured him that we would be most flattered—that we had worked hard to get the doors open and we would be delighted if people knew we existed, etc., etc. Then he said, "The reason I'm asking is that if I write this review it might change your whole life—why, you might have to hire someone just to answer the telephone, because I'm going to say this place is fantastic, and I'm worried for you."

I was elated. So far I had been taking the calls for reservations at the stove on an extra-long cord during the day and Reinhardt was answering the phone from the dining room at night.

The review came out that Sunday. I'll never forget the opening line: "Once in a great while there comes along a restaurant that is so good you worry," and went on to proclaim it the best restaurant in a 150-mile radius of Washington, D.C.

DANIEL MARGOLIS PICNIC

SATURDAY, JULY 6

50 Guests

Fried Chicken

Country Ham

Potato Salad

Deviled Eggs

Sliced Tomatoes Vinaigrette

Corn Muffin Sticks

Naturally all his concerns were well founded. We couldn't eat our granola that morning because the phone wouldn't stop. The callers no longer introduced themselves or had familiar accents. It was even scarier when the day wore on and people started gathering on the porch waiting for us to open. By noon there were already about thirty people, and we didn't open until four. People were pushing themselves against a side door that was secured only by a little dime-store dead bolt. It looked as though they would break through in a matter of minutes and come flooding into the room. I felt that I was having a strange dream or even a nightmare. I chopped the onions for the soup even faster.

As this scene repeated itself again and again, I realized that I needed to function at a pace much faster than I had ever imagined, and without thinking about it, I created a little xylophone of beverages at the stove to keep me flying at the necessary speed. Closest to my left hand was a mug of coffee, which I sipped constantly, and next to it a glass of iced tea if I needed to slow down momentarily. Next in the lineup was a beer if I began to get the shakes or needed to put the brakes on, followed by ice water to ward off dehydration, and lastly some cranberry juice for general nourishment, since I could never remember to eat anything until after the last guests left at midnight.

We raised the prices in self-defense, and the reviews only got better.

At the end of the first year we closed for a winter holiday and went on an expedition to the great restaurants of France, returning home renewed and ready for another year. Initially, the contrast between what we were doing and what we found in France was overwhelming, but as we continued our annual pilgrimages, the gap began to narrow.

After about six years, the public's demands for overnight accommodations had become urgent, and we began to visit the great hotels and inns of the world, beginning with England's great country houses and going all the way to Hong Kong and Bangkok. We made notes of all the little details we liked and tried to incorporate as many of them as possible into the design of our own guest rooms. We had begun working with an architect on the challenging task of turning the old, bat-infested second story and attic into what would resemble an eccentric country house. When we told the architect how concerned we were that the completed rooms should seem to have been here forever, he remembered an artist and set designer he'd gone to school with in London and offered to send her the blueprints to get her ideas.

Soon a large package arrived from England containing fantastical watercolor renderings of the interior spaces, giving them a grandeur beyond our wildest imaginings. Never having had enough money to buy any real art before, we ran to a nearby framer to have these gorgeous watercolors framed to decorate The Inn. The framer wanted to know whose brothel this was. We knew then that we were on the right track.

A jubilant Joyce Evans.

The transformation of the old garage began in earnest, proving that a sow's ear *can* be turned into a silk purse if price is no object. For our British designer, Joyce Evans, fantasy is what life is all about. She had never stepped foot in America, but she was able to conceptualize the designs for all the guest rooms and public spaces simply from architectural blueprints. Joyce purchased almost everything—furniture, fabrics, and wall coverings—in England and numbered it all to be assembled on-site like a giant jigsaw puzzle. This was all happening while the restaurant continued to operate and provide the necessary cash flow for what we were just beginning to realize was a life's work. We were trying to construct just eight guest rooms and complete two suites later in stages. Finally we set an opening date and began to accept reservations.

Two weeks before guests were scheduled to check in, our bank president arrived to tell us that the bank's board had met and decided to cancel our construction loan, making it due and payable by Friday of that week. To no avail, we tried to explain that there was no risk—that deposits for the almost completed rooms were already coming in, but we had to keep paying the construction crew so they could finish the project. It was clear that the situation was bad when we looked up and saw the bank president holding two lit cigarettes—one in each hand. Then he exploded: "Goddamn it, Patrick, you've got to stop operating on blind Christian faith!"

When he left, the reality hit us. We had to come up with a million dollars by Friday. We decided to get up very early the next day and take our accountant with us to big Washington to look for a new bank.

It was bitter cold and windy. We carried Joyce Evans's beautiful drawings with us and trudged up and down K Street, D.C.'s power-banking corridor.

Cold-calling on strange banks is not something I'd recommend. Most of the loan officers looked at us as if we were out of our minds, but we persevered, and finally, as the day was just about over, we knocked on a door and were greeted with: "You're from The Inn at Little Washington? What a coincidence. That's our president's favorite restaurant. Let me see if we can arrange a presentation to our commercial loan committee this afternoon."

They did. They gave us the money. They even suggested we take more than we needed and finish all the rooms as well as two duplex suites on top of the building. (It was the eighties, after all.) We felt as if we had been untied from the railroad track seconds before the locomotive crushed us. We went out for a drink before returning to the country that night.

There were a lot of close calls in those days. In the winter, a country restaurant stays alive on Saturday night's revenues. During January Reinhardt would often tell me on Friday night that if it snowed on Saturday we'd be unable to make our monthly mortgage payment and would probably be bankrupt. I would lie awake listening for the sound of snowflakes on the tin roof. Miraculously it never snowed on Saturday.

Instead, every year brought a flurry of wonderful new awards, along with the added pressure and challenge of living up to them.

Reinhardt Lynch, co-proprietor, and Rose, The Inn's mascot (above).

1

COLD FIRST
COURSES

12 fresh Black Mission figs,
sliced in half lengthwise

2 tablespoons olive oil

1 tablespoon sugar

1 teaspoon ground cinnamon

½ cup heavy cream

¼ cup fresh lime juice

Pinch of freshly grated nutmeg

2 limes

6 ounces Virginia country ham,
thinly sliced

4 teaspoons snipped fresh chives
(optional)

CHILLED GRILLED BLACK MISSION FIGS WITH VIRGINIA COUNTRY HAM AND LIME CREAM

In Virginia, it seems that we are always looking for ways to feature our famous country ham. This is a delightfully simple warm-weather first course to serve when fresh figs come into the market. Grilling or broiling the figs enhances their luscious flavor.

SERVES 4

1. Brush the figs with the oil. 2. In a small bowl, combine the sugar and cinnamon, and sprinkle it over the figs. 3. Preheat the gas grill or broiler. If you're using a grill, lay the figs, flat side down, on the grill rack and heat for 2 to 3 minutes, or until they soften but still hold their shape. If you're using a broiler, place the figs, flat side up, on a lightly oiled baking sheet. Broil them as close to the heating element as possible for 2 to 3 minutes. Remove from the heat and let cool to room temperature. (The figs may be prepared a day in advance and kept refrigerated, but their flavor is far superior when they are served at room temperature.) 4. In the bowl of an electric mixer, whip the cream just until it begins to form soft peaks. Slowly add the lime juice and nutmeg. This mixture should have the consistency of a thick sauce. Place the cream in a pastry bag fitted with a plain tip or in a plastic squeeze bottle and refrigerate.

TO SERVE: 1. Cut the limes in half. Slice a bit off the bottom of each lime half so that it will stand upright. Place one lime half in the center of each of four plates. 2. Arrange six of the figs around each lime. Loosely drape the ham over the figs. Pipe or squeeze the lime cream over the figs and ham in a thin, lacy pattern. If desired, sprinkle each plate with 1 teaspoon of chives.

NOTE: The dish may be fully assembled ahead of time except for the lime cream, which can be made ahead, refrigerated, and added just before serving.

CHILLED CHARCOAL-GRILLED SALMON IN A MUSTARD SEED CRUST

This is a delightfully different treatment for a whole salmon. The fish can be grilled ahead over charcoal outdoors, and makes a beautiful presentation served as a whole side or it can be individually portioned and served chilled as a refreshing summery first course.

Ask your fish supplier to split a whole salmon, removing the head and all the bones but leaving the skin on. The skin will help keep the salmon from falling apart on the grill. Green Herb Mayonnaise (see page 167) and a cucumber salad make excellent accompaniments.

SERVES 8

1 whole salmon, split and boned, with skin (about 3½ pounds)
Salt and freshly ground pepper
1 cup mustard seeds
1 bunch fresh dill, lightly chopped
1 medium-size onion, thinly sliced
¼ cup olive oil

½ pound hickory wood chips (optional)

1. Lay the salmon flesh side up on your work surface. Sprinkle liberally with salt and pepper. Coat with the mustard seed, then the dill and onion slices, and sprinkle with the oil.   **2.** Remove the rack from your charcoal grill and ignite the charcoal. If desired, sprinkle ½ pound of hickory chips on the fire, letting the flames subside to glowing embers.   **3.** Lay the grill rack on top of the fish. Quickly flip the rack over and place the fish over the fire with the skin side facing up. Close the lid on the grill (if it has one) and cook the fish for about 10 minutes.   **4.** Remove the fish from the fire, using tongs or oven mitts to lift the rack, with the fish in place, out of the grill. Set on a large metal tray or baking sheet to cool. Gently remove the skin.

TO SERVE: Place a serving tray or platter on top of the fish and, holding the rack in place, flip the fish over onto the tray. Pick off and discard any burned bits of onion or dill. The salmon may be served whole or cut into strips about 2 inches wide.

Smoked Oyster Canapés with Curry Crème Fraîche

This is one of our favorite canapés. The silky texture of the sweet, brined, smoky oysters is set off by the crunchy toasts and slivered almonds. Smoking your own oysters is a relatively simple procedure, provided you have a gas grill with a lid.

MAKES ABOUT 20 CANAPÉS

TO BRINE OYSTERS: Two days prior to serving, combine the oysters, 2 tablespoons of the brown sugar, and the salt in a 1-quart container. Add enough water to cover and mix well. Refrigerate for 36 to 48 hours.

TO MAKE CURRY CRÈME FRAÎCHE: **1.** In a small saucepan, combine the curry powder, turmeric, and 3 tablespoons of water. Gently heat until the water has evaporated. Remove from the heat and allow to cool. **2.** In a small bowl, combine the crème fraîche or sour cream, curry mixture, and lemon juice. Strain. **3.** Place the strained sauce in a plastic squeeze bottle with a small tip and refrigerate.

TO SMOKE OYSTERS: **1.** Place 1 cup of hickory chips in a small container and cover with warm water. Set aside. **2.** Using a gas or electric grill, preheat the coals to high. Place the soaked chips on the coals and reduce the heat to low. **3.** Remove the oysters from the brine and place on a lightly oiled rack so that they are evenly spaced and do not overlap. **4.** In a small bowl or cup, combine the remaining brown sugar with 2 tablespoons of water. Place beside the grill with a pastry brush. **5.** Place the rack of oysters 2 to 3 inches above the coals and close the lid. Smoke the oysters for about 1 hour, occasionally brushing with the brown sugar and water mixture, until the oysters are firm and light brown.

TO MAKE THE CANAPÉ TOASTS: **1.** Slice the French bread into disks about ⅛ inch thick and place in a single layer on a baking sheet. Place the sheet in a warm place to dry the bread. **2.** In a small saucepan, melt the butter over medium heat until it begins to darken. Remove from the heat. **3.** Preheat the broiler. Toast the French bread rounds under the broiler on both sides. Brush each round with the butter and set aside.

TO SERVE: **1.** Lay the buttered rounds in a single layer on a serving tray. Squeeze a little of the Curry Crème Fraîche on each one, then place an oyster on top. Pipe the remaining curry sauce on the oyster in a spiral pattern. **2.** Garnish each oyster with the almonds and chives.

1 pint fresh oysters, shucked
⅓ cup firmly packed brown sugar
2 tablespoons salt
1 tablespoon curry powder
1 teaspoon ground turmeric
¼ cup crème fraîche or sour cream
1 teaspoon lemon juice
1 small loaf French bread
2 tablespoons butter
½ cup slivered almonds, toasted
2 tablespoons chopped fresh chives

1 cup hickory wood chips (for smoking)

COUNTRY HAM MOUSSE

You'll never throw away another scrap of ham after you see what a delectable mousse you can make from the leftovers and trimmings. Mousse simply means "foam" in French and can be applied to anything having an airy, foamlike texture. The whipped cream in this recipe creates the sensation of the ham literally melting in the mouth.

We pipe the mousse out of a pastry bag fitted with a decorative tip onto toast rounds as a canapé, or spread it into little crocks topped with port jelly and a pecan for an hors d'oeuvre. It also makes a snappy little sandwich spread.

MAKES 24 CANAPÉS

1. Place the ham in a food processor fitted with a steel blade and finely chop.
2. With the processor running, add the sour cream, butter, and the 2 tablespoons cream. Puree until smooth, then transfer to a medium-size bowl. 3. In the bowl of an electric mixer, whip the remaining ½ cup cream until stiff peaks form. 4. With a rubber spatula, fold the cream into the ham puree along with the brandy, pepper, and chives. 5. Store, covered, in the refrigerator until ready to serve.

TO SERVE: Place the mousse in a pastry bag fitted with a decorative tip and pipe onto the toast rounds. Sprinkle with the gherkins and pecans.

NOTE: There is no salt in this recipe because Virginia country ham is preserved with salt. If your ham is also very salty, you may have to add more sour cream to soften the taste. If you feel that the mousse is lacking in salt, by all means add it to taste.

¼ pound country ham
1 tablespoon sour cream
¼ cup (½ stick) unsalted butter
½ cup plus 2 tablespoons heavy cream
1 teaspoon brandy
Freshly ground pepper to taste
3 tablespoons chopped fresh chives
Toast rounds
Minced gherkins
Chopped toasted pecans

NAPOLEON OF POTATO CRISPS, MAINE LOBSTER, AND OSSETRA CAVIAR

This is an elegant, rather dazzling way to present a cold lobster first course when you're feeling a bit extravagant. All the components can be made well in advance and assembled just before serving. Of course you can omit the caviar, but it complements both the lobster and the potato crisps beautifully, and you'll only need 1 ounce to serve four guests, so why not?

We serve this at The Inn on a black plate so that the chopped egg and onion look very dramatic scattered around the napoleons.

SERVES 4

1. Chop the lobster into bite-size pieces, removing any bits of shell or cartilage.
2. Make the potato crisps.   3. In a small bowl, whisk together all the dressing ingredients. Fold the chopped lobster into the dressing, adjust the seasoning, and refrigerate.

TO SERVE: 1. Garnish each of four plates with a sprinkling of chopped egg, onion, chives, and cracked pepper.   2. Spoon a small amount of lobster salad in the center of each plate and top with a potato crisp.   3. Place another spoonful of lobster salad directly on top of the potato crisp and repeat until there are three layers.   4. Top the final potato crisp with a small dollop of crème fraîche or sour cream and one-quarter ounce of the caviar. Garnish the caviar with a parsley leaf.
5. Just before serving, drizzle a few drops of the Tarragon Vinaigrette onto each plate.

POTATO CRISPS

This is a healthful way of making fragile, wafer-thin homemade potato chips in your oven. They come out perfectly flat and can be used to make cocktail "sandwiches" layered with caviar or stacked with a filling such as the lobster napoleon.

MAKES ABOUT 12 CRISPS

1. Preheat the oven to 300 degrees.   2. Peel the potatoes and place in a pan of cold water.   3. In a medium-size saucepan, heat the butter slowly until melted. Skim off the foam and ladle the clear butter into a small saucepan, avoiding the milky residue in the bottom of the pan.   4. Gently heat the clear butter with the garlic for 4 to 5 minutes.   5. Pour a thin layer of butter on a baking sheet and place in the oven.
6. Remove the potatoes from the water. Dry them and slice lengthwise ¹⁄₁₆ inch thick. (Slices will be almost transparent.)   7. Lay the potato slices on the hot baking sheet, leaving a little space between them. Brush the tops liberally with the garlic butter and return to the oven.   8. Rotate the baking sheet every few minutes and

1½-pound lobster, steamed, chilled, and removed from its shell
12 potato crisps (recipe follows)

DRESSING
7 ounces crème fraîche or sour cream
¼ cup mayonnaise
1 medium-size red onion, finely chopped
2 tablespoons peeled, seeded, and chopped tomato
2 tablespoons chopped fresh tarragon
1 tablespoon Dijon mustard
3 tablespoons chopped fresh chives
1 teaspoon capers, drained
1 teaspoon fresh lime juice
½ teaspoon ground cumin
½ teaspoon celery salt
½ teaspoon minced garlic
¼ teaspoon cayenne pepper
Salt and freshly ground pepper to taste

GARNISHES
1 hard-boiled egg, finaely chopped
1 medium size red onion, finely chopped
2 tablespoons chopped fresh chives
Freshly cracked pepper
1 ounce crème fraîche or sour cream
1 ounce fresh Ossetra caviar
4 leaves Italian parsley
2 tablespoons Tarragon Vinaigrette (see page 166)

3 large Idaho potatoes
1 pound (4 sticks) lightly salted butter
6 cloves garlic, peeled
Salt to taste

1 pound very fresh tuna

MARINADE

2 tablespoons soy sauce

¼ cup rice wine vinegar

2 teaspoons toasted sesame oil

½ teaspoon freshly ground black pepper

Pinch of cayenne pepper

WASABI MAYONNAISE

1 tablespoon wasabi (Japanese horseradish) powder

2 tablespoons warm water

1 cup homemade mayonnaise or good quality store-bought

1 teaspoon fresh lemon juice

TARTARE

3 ounces toasted sesame seeds (about 4 tablespoons)

3 tablespoons chopped fresh chives

2 tablespoons chopped fresh cilantro

Freshly ground pepper to taste

GARNISHES

2 tablespoons toasted sesame oil

2 tablespoons toasted sesame seeds

½ fresh lime

turn the crisps over with a spatula when they begin to brown on the edges. **9.** When the crisps are an even golden brown, remove from the oven and drain on paper towels. Sprinkle lightly with salt while still warm. **10.** Continue the process, using the same baking sheet, until all the potato slices are cooked. The crisps may be layered between paper towels, wrapped tightly, and stored for several days at room temperature.

FRESH TUNA TARTARE ON TUNA CARPACCIO WITH WASABI MAYONNAISE

This is a great way to use trimmings from tuna steaks. Be sure to ask for very freshest "sushi quality" tuna. Either the tartare or the carpaccio can be served by itself, but they're more interesting in combination. The wasabi mayonnaise brings all the flavors together.

SERVES 4

FOR THE CARPACCIO: Slice four 1-ounce pieces from the tuna and place each slice between two sheets of lightly oiled waxed paper. Using a large wooden spoon or the flat side of a wooden mallet, pound each piece until nearly transparent. Stack the paper-wrapped tuna on a plate and refrigerate.

FOR THE TARTARE: Mince the remaining tuna, being careful to remove any sinew or dark patches, and put in a covered bowl in the refrigerator.

TO MAKE THE MARINADE: Combine all the ingredients for the marinade in a jar with a tight-fitting lid and refrigerate until ready to use. This marinade may be made several days in advance.

TO MAKE THE MAYONNAISE: In a small bowl, combine the wasabi powder with the warm water and stir until a smooth paste forms. Whisk in the mayonnaise and the lemon juice. Place in a plastic squeeze bottle with a small tip and refrigerate.

TO ASSEMBLE: 1. Remove the tartare from the refrigerator. Shake the marinade well and pour on just enough to moisten the tuna, mixing well with a fork. **2.** Sprinkle 2 tablespoons of the sesame seeds, the chives, and the cilantro into the mixture. Season with pepper. **3.** Sprinkle 1 teaspoon of the remaining sesame seeds in each of four 3-ounce ramekins. Pack the tartare mixture tightly into the ramekins.

TO SERVE: 1. Brush the rim of a decorative plate (black if possible) with a little sesame oil and sprinkle the rim with toasted sesame seeds. Squeeze a little lime juice on the plate. **2.** Carefully peel the waxed paper off the carpaccio and place on the center of each plate. Make a fanciful latticework design across the carpaccio with the wasabi mayonnaise. **3.** Unmold the tartare on top of the carpaccio. Serve with decorative chopsticks and something crispy like wasabi chips.

2 boneless lamb loins or 1 rack of lamb
(if you're using the rack, carefully
remove the entire loin from the bone
using a small, sharp knife)
1 tablespoon dried tarragon
1 tablespoon dried thyme
1 tablespoon dried oregano
1 tablespoon dried basil
Salt and freshly ground pepper
2 tablespoons olive oil
2 bunches arugula
1 fresh mint leaf
2 teaspoons capers, drained

MUSTARD-ROSEMARY SAUCE
½ cup olive oil
1 sprig fresh rosemary
½ cup mayonnaise
2 tablespoons Dijon mustard
1 teaspoon lemon juice
1 teaspoon chopped fresh rosemary

TABOULI
¼ cup water
2 tablespoons bulgur
1 teaspoon chopped fresh mint
1 teaspoon chopped fresh parsley
1 teaspoon chopped shallot
1 tablespoon olive oil
1 teaspoon peeled, seeded,
and chopped tomato
½ teaspoon minced garlic
1 tablespoon lemon juice
Salt and freshly ground pepper to taste

CARPACCIO OF BABY LAMB ON ARUGULA WITH MUSTARD-ROSEMARY SAUCE AND TABOULI

The traditional carpaccio of beef was first created on a hot night many years ago at Harry's Bar in Venice, Italy. It was named after the painter Vittore Carpaccio, who was known for his vibrant red and ocher sunsets, which the raw meat resembles (if you squint). This version, which uses lamb, is the best of both worlds in that the interior is still raw, but the exterior is coated with pepper and herbs and seared, giving it much more flavor than the completely raw beef original.

SERVES 6

1. Trim the loin of any fat or sinew.   2. Place a large iron skillet over high heat.
3. In a small bowl, combine the tarragon, thyme, oregano, and basil.   4. Sprinkle the lamb heavily with salt and pepper and completely coat with the herb mixture.
5. Drizzle the loins with the 1 tablespoon oil and place in the hot skillet one at a time. Roll each loin in the pan just enough to sear the exterior, allowing only the herbs to darken.   6. Remove the loins from the skillet, allow to come to room temperature, and wrap tightly in plastic wrap, squeezing the loins into perfect cylinders. Place the wrapped loins in the freezer for about 2 hours, or until frozen solid.

TO MAKE THE SAUCE: 1. In a small saucepan, heat the oil and the sprig of rosemary until the rosemary begins to darken. Remove the rosemary and let the oil cool to room temperature.   2. In a medium-size stainless steel bowl, whisk together the mayonnaise and mustard. While still whisking, pour in the rosemary-flavored oil in a thin stream, incorporating thoroughly. Whisk in the lemon juice and chopped rosemary. Pour the sauce into a squeeze bottle fitted with a narrow tip and refrigerate.

TO MAKE THE TABOULI: 1. In a small saucepan, bring the water to a boil. Place the bulgur in a small bowl and pour the boiling water over it. Let soften for about 20 minutes.   2. Drain off any excess water and stir in the mint, parsley, shallot, oil, tomato, garlic, lemon juice, salt, and pepper.

TO SERVE: 1. Remove the lamb from the freezer and allow to defrost slightly, about 5 minutes.   2. Toss the arugula leaves in the remaining oil and arrange on a plate in three clusters.   3. Squeeze the Mustard-Rosemary Sauce onto the plate in a lacy loop pattern.   4. Slice the loins as thinly as possible with a sharp chef's knife and arrange the slices in a circular pattern on top of the arugula. (The slices will defrost almost immediately.)   5. Place 1 tablespoon of tabouli in the center of the circle and garnish with a mint leaf. Sprinkle the capers on the plate.

2 veal butt tenderloins,
approximately 1 pound each
Salt and freshly ground pepper to taste
2 tablespoons fresh thyme
Olive oil

TONNATO SAUCE
8 ounces fresh tuna (grilled or broiled to
medium) cooled and flaked
2 egg yolks
4 canned anchovies
4 tablespoons capers, drained
1½ cups olive oil
½ cup heavy cream
¼ cup fresh lemon juice
Salt and freshly ground pepper to taste

TOMATO-CAPER SALSA
½ cup peeled, seeded, and chopped fresh
or canned tomato
¼ cup capers, drained
2 tablespoons minced shallot
½ teaspoon chopped garlic
½ teaspoon chopped fresh thyme
1 tablespoon balsamic vinegar
1 teaspoon fresh lemon juice
1 teaspoon extra-virgin olive oil
Salt and freshly ground pepper to taste

GARNISHES
6 black olives, preferably niçoise,
pitted and julienned
2 tablespoons capers, drained
2 tablespoons chopped fresh chives
Fresh thyme sprigs

VITELLO TONNATO

In Italian, vitello *means "veal" and* tonnato *means "tuna." The traditional version of this dish uses a braised veal shoulder served chilled with a sauce of pureed canned tuna packed in olive oil. Our adaptation uses grilled veal butt tenderloins, which can be prepared in minutes, and a sauce made with grilled fresh tuna. The dish is served cool and can be prepared well in advance. It is a lovely first course for an Italian menu and makes an ideal buffet dish.*

SERVES 6

TO PREPARE THE VEAL: 1. Rub tenderloins with salt, pepper, and thyme leaves.   2. Coat lightly with olive oil and grill to medium rare. Set aside.

TO MAKE THE TONNATO SAUCE: In a food processor puree the tuna, egg yolks, anchovies, and capers. With the processor running, slowly add the oil until emulsified. Add the cream and lemon juice. Season with salt and pepper.

TO MAKE THE SALSA: Mix all ingredients together.

TO SERVE: 1. Slice the veal about ¼ inch thick and arrange in a flower pattern in the center of a chilled plate.   2. Spoon the tuna sauce around the veal to cover the entire plate   3. Sprinkle the olives, capers, and chives over the sauce. 4. Spoon the salsa onto the center of the veal and garnish with a fresh thyme sprig.

Marinated Shiitake Mushrooms with Chilled Vermicelli

Having three shiitake mushroom farms in our area has inspired us to create ideas for using them in quantity. Cooked in a marinade and served chilled or at room temperature, the mushrooms work well as a first course on noodles for a warm-weather dinner, make a wonderful buffet dish, and are perfect to take on a picnic. The mixture will keep for a good while refrigerated and is great to have on hand as a condiment to enhance anything from steak to hamburger.

TO PREPARE THE MUSHROOMS:
1. In a 6-quart saucepan over medium heat, combine the tomatoes, tomato paste, balsamic vinegar, red wine vinegar, thyme, herbes de Provence (if using), sugar, salt and pepper, and Tabasco. Bring to a boil and reduce the heat to a simmer. **2.** Meanwhile, heat ¼ cup of the oil in a heavy skillet over medium heat and add the onion slices. Cook, stirring constantly, until wilted. **3.** Add the onions to the tomato mixture and cook, stirring occasionally, for about 30 minutes, or until the sauce is quite thick. Stir in the garlic and remove from the heat. **4.** Remove the stems from the mushrooms and slice the caps into strips about ½ inch thick. There should be about 10 cups. **5.** In a heavy skillet over medium heat, sauté the mushrooms in two batches in the remaining oil for 4 to 5 minutes, or until crisp. Add to the tomato mixture. Let stand at room temperature.

TO PREPARE THE NOODLES: **1.** Bring a large quantity of salted water to a boil in a large pot. Add the vermicelli and cook until al dente, about 3 minutes. Do not overcook. **2.** Drain the noodles and run under cold water until chilled. Drain thoroughly. **3.** Pour the noodles into a large bowl. Add the olive oil, scallions or chives, sesame oil, soy sauce, garlic, ginger, and five-spice powder. Toss to blend well.

TO SERVE: Make a nest of the noodles on a platter and place a mound of the marinated mushrooms in the center. Serve at cool room temperature.

MARINATED MUSHROOMS
2½ cups peeled, seeded, and cubed fresh or canned tomatoes
¼ cup tomato paste
1 tablespoon balsamic vinegar
⅓ cup red wine vinegar
2½ teaspoons dried thyme
½ teaspoon herbes de Provence (optional)
3 tablespoons sugar
Salt and freshly ground pepper to taste
¼ teaspoon Tabasco
1 cup extra-virgin olive oil
2 cups thinly sliced onions, loosely packed
2 teaspoons minced garlic
1¼ pounds shiitake mushrooms

NOODLES
4 ounces vermicelli
2 tablespoons extra-virgin olive oil
2 tablespoons finely chopped scallions or fresh chives
½ tablespoon sesame oil
1 teaspoon soy sauce
¼ teaspoon minced garlic
¼ teaspoon grated fresh ginger
⅛ teaspoon five-spice powder

2

HOT FIRST
COURSES

Risotto with Shrimp, Oyster Mushrooms, and Country Ham

Here is a restaurant trick for making risotto that allows you to partially cook the rice in advance and chill it to prevent overcooking. It can then be quickly reheated and finished by adding hot liquid just before serving. The rice will remain beautifully al dente. Not even an Italian grandmother will be able to discern that you performed all the time-consuming procedures a day in advance.

Serves 8

TO MAKE THE RISOTTO BASE: **1.** In a 2-quart saucepan, bring the stock or water to a boil over high heat. Reduce the heat and keep just below boiling. **2.** In another 2-quart saucepan, heat the butter and oil. Add the onion and cook until translucent. Add the mushrooms, stirring with a wooden spoon, and cook for about 4 minutes more. **3.** Add the rice and stir until it is evenly coated with the butter-oil mixture. **4.** Slowly add the hot stock, ⅔ cup at a time, stirring constantly until the rice absorbs the liquid. This should take about 4 to 5 minutes for each addition. **5.** When all the stock has been absorbed, remove the risotto from the stove and pour onto a baking sheet to stop the cooking and cool as quickly as possible. (The rice will still taste a bit raw in the center.) Refrigerate, uncovered, until cold. (The risotto base can then be stored in a covered plastic container for up to 2 days.)

TO PREPARE THE RISOTTO, SHRIMP, AND MUSHROOMS: **1.** Bring the stock or water to a boil. **2.** Place the chilled risotto base in a 4-quart saucepan over medium heat and add the butter. Pour 1½ cups of the boiling stock slowly into the risotto, stirring constantly with a wooden spoon. Continue cooking until the rice is just barely tender but still al dente. **3.** Stir in the cheese, adjusting the consistency with more stock if the risotto becomes too thick. Remove from the heat and keep warm. **4.** In a 10-inch sauté pan, heat 2 tablespoons of the oil almost to smoking. Add the shrimp and sauté until just pink, being careful not to overcook. Add a pinch of the shallot and garlic and sauté for a few seconds more. Season with salt and pepper, remove from the pan, and keep warm. **5.** In the same skillet, heat the remaining 2 tablespoons oil until very hot. Add the mushrooms and sauté. Add the remaining shallot and garlic. Season with salt and pepper and remove from the pan.

TO SERVE: Divide the risotto into eight warm soup plates. Sprinkle the shrimp and mushrooms on top of each portion. Garnish with the cheese, ham, and chives.

RISOTTO BASE
2 cups shellfish stock, chicken stock, or water

2 tablespoons butter

2 tablespoons olive oil

½ large onion, minced

1 cup oyster mushrooms, coarsely chopped

1 cup Arborio rice

SHRIMP AND MUSHROOMS
1½ cups shellfish stock, chicken stock, or water (approximately)

½ cup (1 stick) butter

1 cup freshly grated Parmesan or Asiago cheese

4 tablespoons olive oil

24 fresh shrimp, peeled, deveined, and split in half lengthwise

1 teaspoon minced shallot

½ teaspoon minced garlic

Salt and freshly ground pepper to taste

1 cup oyster mushrooms, coarsely chopped

GARNISHES
Freshly grated Parmesan or Asiago cheese

½ cup julienned country ham

1 tablespoon chopped fresh chives

1 tablespoon butter

1 tablespoon chopped shallot

½ bay leaf

1 cup fresh blackberries

½ cup water

½ cup cassis

2 tablespoons currant jelly

2 tablespoons chicken stock, preferably homemade (see page 170)

½ teaspoon finely chopped fresh thyme

Freshly ground pepper to taste

POLENTA

1 tablespoon butter

4 tablespoons olive oil

½ teaspoon minced garlic

1 bay leaf

½ cup water

½ cup milk

½ cup heavy cream

¼ cup yellow cornmeal

¼ cup freshly grated Parmesan or Asiago cheese

Salt and cayenne pepper to taste

FOIE GRAS

1 foie gras, about 1¼ pounds

Salt and freshly ground pepper to taste

1 pint fresh blackberries

2 cups mixed greens, such as watercress, frisée, or red oak lettuce

Extra-virgin olive oil

8 very thin slices country ham, trimmed of fat and cut into 2-inch squares

2 tablespoons chopped fresh chives

CRISPY SEARED FOIE GRAS ON POLENTA WITH COUNTRY HAM AND BLACKBERRIES

This is one of our most popular first courses. The combination of flavors is tantalizing—definitely worth blowing the budget to purchase foie gras (fattened duck liver; see Note). When cooking foie gras, it's very important to use a smoking-hot pan; otherwise the liver will just melt away like butter. You want to create a crisp exterior and a rare interior. Foie gras must be eaten within seconds after it's cooked, or it will be flabby.

SERVES 8

TO MAKE THE SAUCE: **1.** In a 2-quart saucepan, melt the butter over low heat. Add the shallot, bay leaf, and blackberries and sweat for 3 minutes. **2.** Add the water, cassis, jelly, and stock. Simmer over medium heat for about 30 minutes, or until the sauce is the consistency of a light syrup. **3.** Remove from the heat and add the thyme and pepper. Set aside for 10 minutes. Strain.

TO MAKE THE POLENTA: **1.** In a 4-quart saucepan, melt the butter over low heat. Add 1 tablespoon of the oil, the garlic, and bay leaf and sweat for 30 seconds. **2.** Add the water, milk, and cream and bring to a simmer. Remove the bay leaf. **3.** Whisking constantly, add the cornmeal. Simmer for 2 minutes, or until the polenta begins to thicken. **4.** Whisk in the cheese and season with salt and cayenne. **5.** Line a baking sheet with plastic wrap and pour the polenta onto the sheet. Cover with plastic wrap and flatten to about ½ inch thick. Refrigerate for 1 hour. **6.** Remove from the refrigerator and cut into 2-inch squares. Sauté both sides in the remaining oil until golden brown. Keep warm.

TO PREPARE THE FOIE GRAS: **1.** Soak the foie gras in a bowl of ice water for 10 minutes to draw out the blood and firm up the flesh. **2.** Separate the two lobes of the liver, removing any fat or sinew. **3.** Using a very sharp knife dipped in warm water, slice the liver on the bias into ¼-inch slices. Season with salt and pepper. **4.** In a heavy skillet, sear the foie gras over high heat for about 30 seconds on each side, or just until a golden brown crust forms. Remove from the skillet and blot on paper towels. **5.** Pour off the excess fat and deglaze the pan with the reserved blackberry sauce. Add the fresh blackberries and reduce the sauce to a syrupy consistency.

TO SERVE: **1.** In a medium-size bowl, toss the greens with the oil and salt and pepper. Place a small bouquet of dressed greens in the center of each of eight warm serving plates. **2.** Place a square of polenta on top of the greens. Then place a slice of ham on top of the polenta. Top with one piece of foie gras. **3.** Spoon the sauce over the liver. Sprinkle with the chives.

NOTE: To avoid wasting even a morsel of the costly foie gras, slice the entire liver and freeze whatever you don't need for the recipe. Simply lay the slices out on a baking sheet lined with plastic wrap. When thoroughly frozen, the slices may be individually wrapped and stored in the freezer. Whenever you have a craving for foie gras, just toss the frozen slices directly into a hot pan. They'll cook beautifully.

SCALLOPS BAKED IN THEIR SHELLS WITH SAUTERNES AND BLACK TRUFFLE

Most people have never seen a live scallop in the shell. Your fish supplier will probably have to special-order them for you. Scallops are usually opened on the fishing boats and chemically treated to give them a longer shelf life. Live scallops in the shell are far more perishable. But once you've tasted the difference, you'll find it hard to go back to preshucked scallops.

Female scallops sometimes contain roe—a small elliptical egg sack, which connoisseurs consider a delicacy. When cooked, it turns a lovely pink color. In this preparation, the scallops are pried open and the flesh is removed, sliced, and put back into the cleaned shells along with brightly colored julienned peppers, a splash of sweet wine, a bit of butter, and optional slices of fresh black truffle. The shell is resealed with mashed potatoes. (All of this preparation can be done a day in advance.) Just before serving, the scallops are popped into a hot oven for 7 to 8 minutes. They're presented on a bed of seaweed and opened at the table, giving off a burst of heavenly aromas.

SERVES 6

TO MAKE THE TARRAGON BUTTER: In a small bowl, combine the butter, 2 tablespoons of the sauternes, and the tarragon. Set aside.

TO PREPARE THE SCALLOPS: 1. Preheat the oven to 425 degrees. 2. Using an oyster knife, gently pry open each scallop shell. Using a sharp paring knife, remove the large white scallop from the shell and drop into a bowl of ice water. 4. Thoroughly scrub the shells, keeping the matched tops and bottoms together. Lightly butter the interior of the bottom shells with tarragon butter. One tablespoon should be enough to coat all six shells. 5. Remove the scallop from the ice water and trim off any remaining connective membrane. Cut each scallop horizontally into 3 slices and place the slices fanned out, in the bottom half of a buttered shell. 6. Cut the truffle (if using) into very thin slices and place a slice of truffle on each scallop slice. 7. Sprinkle each scallop with salt and white pepper, then distribute the julienned peppers among the scallops. Place 1 tablespoon of the remaining tarragon butter on top of the peppers and pour 1 tablespoon of the remaining sauternes into each shell. 8. Fill a pastry bag fitted with a plain tip with the Garlic Mashed Potatoes and pipe a ¼-inch band of potato around the rim of each bottom shell. Set the matching top shell in place on the potato and press firmly to create a tight seal. Remove any potato that has squeezed out from the sides of the shells. 9. Place the scallops on a baking sheet and bake in the middle of the oven for 6 to 8 minutes.

TO SERVE: If desired, arrange a nest of seaweed on each of six serving plates and place the baked scallops (still sealed in their shells) on top. Invite your guests to open the scallops by inserting a table knife into the mashed potatoes, breaking the seal and releasing the fragrant aromas.

TARRAGON BUTTER
7 tablespoons unsalted butter, softened
8 tablespoons sauternes
1 teaspoon finely chopped fresh tarragon

6 live jumbo Maine sea scallops in the shell
1 fresh black truffle (optional)
Salt and white pepper to taste
¼ cup julienned red bell pepper
¼ cup julienned yellow bell pepper
¼ cup julienned green bell pepper
½ recipe Garlic Mashed Potatoes (see page 119)
1 pound seaweed, blanched, refreshed in ice water, and drained (optional; see Note at top of page 26)

Nonstick cooking spray
Basic Pie Dough (see page 157)

CARAMELIZED ONIONS
2 tablespoons unsalted butter
2 medium-size onions, preferably
Vidalia, very thinly sliced
1 teaspoon sugar

CUSTARD
3 eggs
¾ cup heavy cream
2 tablespoons Dijon mustard
Pinch of celery salt
Pinch of cayenne pepper

MINIATURE CARAMELIZED ONION TARTLETS

These are among the simplest but most delicious savory little hors d'oeuvres in our repertoire. The onions can be caramelized days in advance and kept refrigerated. The pastry shells can be baked and stored in the freezer for up to a week, and the custard mixture can be made well in advance and refrigerated. Last-minute assembly and baking should take less than 20 minutes.

MAKES 24 TARTLETS

1. Lightly spray 2 gem pans or mini muffin tins with nonstick cooking spray. **2.** Roll the dough out evenly on a floured board to about ⅛ inch thick. Using a 3-inch round cookie cutter, stamp out 24 circles of dough. Line the inside of each muffin cup with a dough round, using your fingertips to press it into shape.   **3.** Fill each cup with pie weights or dried beans and chill for 30 minutes.   **4.** Preheat the oven to 350 degrees.   **5.** Bake the shells for 6 minutes. Remove from the oven and cool in the pans.   **6.** When the shells are cool, invert the pans onto a baking sheet. Pick out any remaining pie weights or beans and save for future use.

TO MAKE THE CARAMELIZED ONIONS: 1. In a heavy-bottomed saucepan, melt the butter over medium heat. Add the onion slices and cook, stirring, until wilted. Reduce the heat and cook, stirring frequently, until the onions develop a rich golden color.   **2.** Add the sugar and continue cooking until the onions are the color of brown sugar. Remove from the heat and set aside.

TO MAKE THE CUSTARD: In a small bowl, whisk together the eggs, cream, mustard, celery salt, and cayenne.

TO ASSEMBLE: 1. Preheat the oven to 350 degrees.   **2.** Place ½ teaspoon of the caramelized onions in each pastry shell. Cover the onions with the custard. **3.** Place the tartlets on a wire rack set on a baking sheet. (This allows for a more even distribution of the heat and creates a crisper pastry.) Bake for 10 minutes, or until the custard is just set.

Fresh Tuna Cakes

These savory little tuna cakes make perfect canapés on toast rounds. Shaped slightly bigger, they're also a delightful first course or lunch dish (serve on a bun with lettuce, tomato, and a flavored mayonnaise). We feature these as a first course at The Inn, together with salmon and crab cakes in a potato nest with three differently flavored mayonnaises. This is an excellent way to use up any leftover pieces or trimmings from tuna steaks.

SERVES 4 TO 6

1. Grill or broil the tuna until cooked through but not dry. Cool to room temperature.   2. In a medium-size bowl, flake the tuna into very small pieces with a fork. Stir in the onion, capers, dill, cornichons or gherkins, and olives. Fold in the mayonnaise and lemon juice. Season with salt and pepper.   3. Form the tuna mixture into patties. Place them on a baking sheet and refrigerate. (The tuna cakes may be made up to a day in advance.)   4. Just before serving, dust the tuna cakes with flour. Pour ¼ inch of oil into a sauté pan or heavy skillet and heat almost to smoking. (Frying the cakes in very hot oil allows them to form a crisp exterior without absorbing too much oil.) Add the tuna cakes to the pan and brown on both sides. Remove and drain on paper towels.

TO SERVE: Serve the tuna cakes with with Mustard Mayonnaise on the side.

1 pound fresh tuna
2 tablespoons minced red onion
1 tablespoon capers, drained
2 tablespoons finely chopped fresh dill
3 tablespoons finely chopped cornichons or gherkins
1 tablespoon pitted and chopped black olives, preferably niçoise
3 tablespoons mayonnaise, preferably homemade
1 tablespoon fresh lemon juice
Salt and freshly ground pepper to taste
½ cup all-purpose flour
½ cup olive oil
Mustard Mayonnaise (see page 167)

3 sets fresh shad roe

Salt and freshly ground pepper to taste

½ cup all-purpose flour (approximately)

1 cup clarified butter

½ cup plus Brown Butter (see page 169)

2 tablespoons lemon juice

3 slightly underripe bananas

3 cups fresh spinach, stems removed

1 tablespoon butter

Pinch of white pepper

Pinch of sugar

Pinch of freshly grated nutmeg

*Chardonnay Butter Sauce
(see page 169)*

SHAD ROE WITH BANANA SAUTÉ AND CHARDONNAY BUTTER SAUCE

Admittedly, this is a bizarre-sounding combination, but once you've tried it, you'll be surprised at how well the flavors and textures complement each other. The banana imparts a pleasant sweetness to the shad roe and strongly resembles it in consistency. The butter sauce is optional but definitely adds a bit of sensuality that is well worth the caloric intake.

SERVES 6

1. Remove the connecting membranes from the roe and divide into individual lobes. Season with salt and pepper and dust with flour. **2.** Preheat the oven to 450 degrees. **3.** In a sauté pan, lightly sauté the roe in the clarified butter. Turn over and place the pan in the oven for 1 to 2 minutes, or until the roe are barely firm. **4.** Remove the roe from the pan. Reserve the clarified butter in the pan. Baste each piece of roe lightly with the Brown Butter and lemon juice. **5.** Peel the bananas and cut on the bias into ¼-inch slices. Dredge the slices with flour and quickly sauté in the remaining clarified butter over high heat until golden brown and crisp.

TO SERVE: 1. Wilt the spinach in a saucepan with the tablespoon of butter and season with browned butter, salt, white pepper, sugar, and nutmeg. **2.** Ladle a small pool of the Chardonnay Butter Sauce onto each of six serving plates. Place one piece of shad roe on the sauce. Lay the sautéed banana slices on top of the roe in a fish scale pattern. Serve immediately.

4 small to medium-size soft-shell crabs

⅓ cup coarsely chopped hazelnuts, toasted

1 tablespoon chopped fresh cilantro

1 ripe tomato, peeled, seeded, and diced

Salt and freshly ground pepper to taste

½ cup all-purpose flour

¼ cup clarified butter

2 tablespoons Brown Butter
(see page 169)

Juice of 1 lime

GARNISHES

16 very thin French green beans
(haricots verts), blanched, refreshed in
ice water, drained, and dried

¼ cup vinaigrette

1 lime, peeled, pith removed,
and cut into sections

Fresh cilantro leaves

Mustard Mayonnaise (see page 167)

2 tablespoons chopped fresh chives

SOFT-SHELL CRAB SAUTÉ WITH TOMATO, CILANTRO, LIME, AND HAZELNUTS

Soft-shell crabs are surprisingly quick and easy to prepare at home. The only difficulty is finding them. Frozen crabs are not a happy substitute. We look for the tiniest, freshest ones available. Ideally you should purchase soft shells still kicking.

The crunch of the green beans and hazelnuts in this rendition makes the shells seem even softer.

SERVES 4

1. Clean the crabs by lifting up the side flaps and pulling out the feathery gills. Remove the flap underneath. Rinse in cold water and dry on paper towels. **2.** Preheat the oven to 400 degrees. **3.** In a small bowl, combine the hazelnuts, chopped cilantro, and tomato. **4.** Season each crab with salt and pepper. Place the flour in a shallow dish. Dredge each crab lightly and evenly in the flour, shaking off any excess. **5.** Heat the clarified butter in a heavy-bottomed 12-inch sauté pan over medium-high heat. When the butter is hot but not smoking, carefully place the crabs in the pan, shell side down. Turn the crabs when their shells have blistered. **6.** Add the mixture of hazelnuts, cilantro, and tomatoes and the Brown Butter to the pan. Place the pan in the oven and bake for 2 to 3 minutes, or until the meat under the shells turns white. **7.** Remove the crabs to a platter, pouring the pan juices over them. Drizzle with the lime juice and keep warm. **8.** Cut the green beans into 1½-inch lengths. In a small stainless steel or glass bowl, toss the beans with the vinaigrette.

TO SERVE: 1. On each of four serving plates, make a little nest of crisscrossed beans. Place one hot crab on top of the beans. Place or scatter lime sections and cilantro leaves on top of each crab. **2.** Using a squirt bottle, drizzle the Mustard Mayonnaise in an interesting pattern on the plate. Garnish with the chives.

HALF-SEARED TUNA, SALMON, AND SEA SCALLOPS IN A FRAGRANT CILANTRO AND LIME ESSENCE

This is a stunning, Oriental-inspired presentation of briefly marinated morsels of seafood that are seared on the exterior and rare in the center. The half-seared cubes of fish are sliced in half to display their interiors and are presented on black plates brushed with sesame oil and coated with sesame seeds. The sauce is a wonderfully versatile, Vietnamese-style clear fish sauce with practically no calories—one that you will definitely want to include in your repertoire. Shrimp may be substituted for the tuna or salmon, as shown in the photograph opposite.

SERVES 6

TO MAKE THE MARINADE: Combine ingredients for the marinade in a jar with a tight-fitting lid. Shake well and refrigerate.

TO PREPARE THE PLATES: Dip a pastry brush in the sesame oil and paint a thin coating of oil on the rim of six serving plates (preferably black). Sprinkle the sesame seeds on the oil, coating the rim.

TO PREPARE THE NOODLES AND FISH: 1. Bring 4 cups of water to a boil in a medium-size saucepan. Remove from the heat and add the noodles. Let sit for 8 to 10 minutes, or until tender. 2. Drain the noodles and place in a medium-size bowl. Add the three bell peppers and toss with ½ cup of the fish sauce. 3. Place a small mound of the seasoned noodles and peppers in the center of each serving plate. 4. Remove the marinade from the refrigerator, shake well, and pour into a medium-size bowl. Place the tuna, salmon, and scallops in the marinade and let sit for 5 minutes. Drain the fish and brush lightly with the vegetable oil. Sprinkle the tuna cubes with the remaining black pepper. 5. Set a cast-iron skillet over very high heat. 6. Place several pieces of fish in the skillet and sear for about 30 seconds on all sides, turning the cubes with tongs. Remove from the pan, keep warm, and continue until all the fish is seared.

TO SERVE: 1. Using a very sharp knife, slice each piece of seafood carefully in half crosswise and place one whole sliced scallop, one piece of sliced tuna, and one piece of sliced salmon around the mound of noodles on each plate, fanning them slightly to show the rare interior of each. 2. Moisten the plates with the remaining ½ cup fish sauce and serve immediately.

MARINADE

1 cup soy sauce

Juice of 1 lemon

¼ cup dry sherry

2 tablespoons minced fresh ginger

¼ cup chopped scallions

½ teaspoon cayenne pepper

2 tablespoons freshly ground pepper

¼ cup toasted sesame oil

½ cup toasted sesame seeds

1 small package oriental cellophane noodles (dried bean thread)

⅓ cup julienned red bell pepper

⅓ cup julienned yellow bell pepper

⅓ cup julienned green bell pepper

¾ pound fresh tuna, trimmed, skinned, and cut into 1½-inch cubes

¾ pound fresh salmon, trimmed, skinned, and cut into 1½-inch cubes

6 large sea scallops, rinsed and dried

¼ cup vegetable oil

1 cup Clear Fish Sauce with Lime and Cilantro (see page 168)

TIMBALES OF FRESH CRABMEAT AND SPINACH MOUSSE

Crabmeat is one of our region's great natural delicacies. This dish first appeared on our menu in 1978 and has become a classic. While very delicate (Mimi Sheraton called it "cloud-like"), it is substantial enough to be served as a main course for an elegant luncheon.

SERVES 8

TO MAKE THE MOUSSE: **1.** In a 2-quart heavy-bottomed saucepan over medium heat, melt the butter. Add the flour, and stir with a wooden spoon for 3 to 4 minutes or until the flour turns a light golden brown. Remove from the heat. **2.** In a 1-quart heavy-bottomed saucepan, scald the milk and cream. Remove from the heat and add to the flour mixture, whisking to incorporate. **3.** Place over medium heat and cook, stirring frequently, until mixture is very thick. Remove from the heat. **4.** Blanch the spinach in rapidly boiling water for 30 seconds. Drain, pressing out any excess liquid. Add to the thickened cream mixture. **5.** Puree the spinach sauce in a blender or food processor until smooth. Add the eggs and blend lightly to just incorporate. (Do not over whip the spinach puree.) Add the nutmeg, white pepper, and salt. The mousse can be stored in the refrigerator for up to several days.

NOTE: Any vegetable mousse can be made with this procedure by substituting 1 cup of the vegetable puree of your choice for the spinach.

TO MAKE THE CUSTARD: In a stainless steel bowl, whisk together the eggs, cream, and mustard. Season with the celery salt, cayenne pepper, and salt. The egg mixture can be stored in the refrigerator for up to two days.

TO ASSEMBLE: **1.** Pick through the crabmeat carefully to be sure that all the shell and cartilage are removed. **2.** Preheat the oven to 350 degrees. **3.** Put 2 quarts of water on to boil. **4.** Brush eight 5-ounce timbale molds with clarified butter. Cut out eight round disks of waxed paper and place one in the bottom of each mold. Brush the paper with butter. **5.** Divide the crabmeat among the eight molds. Pour 2 tablespoons of the custard over the crabmeat in each mold. Carefully fill the molds with the mousse. **6.** Place the filled molds in a 12- by 12- by 2-inch baking dish. Fill the dish halfway with boiling water and place gently on the lower rack of the oven. Bake for 50 to 60 minutes, or until the mousse is firm to the touch. If the tops of the timbales begin to brown, cover with aluminum foil. **7.** Carefully remove the dish from the oven and let the timbales set a bit. (The timbales can be kept in a warm water bath on top of the stove for several hours.)

ROASTED RED PEPPER GARNISH: Char 1 large red bell pepper over an open flame or broil in the oven until blackened on all sides. Wrap the pepper in aluminum foil and cool for 30 minutes. This allows the pepper to "sweat," making it easier to peel. Peel, split, and seed the pepper. Using a small decorative cutter (1 inch or less in diameter), cut out eight garnishes.

SPINACH MOUSSE
1 tablespoon butter
1 tablespoon all-purpose flour
½ cup milk
1 cup heavy cream
2 quarts fresh spinach, stems removed
4 eggs
Pinch of freshly grated nutmeg
Pinch of white pepper
Salt to taste

EGG CUSTARD
3 eggs
½ cup heavy cream
1 tablespoon Dijon mustard
Celery salt to taste
Cayenne pepper to taste
Salt to taste

½ pound jumbo lump crabmeat
Clarified butter

Chardonnay Butter Sauce
(see page 169)

GARNISH
1 large red bell pepper

TO SERVE: **1.** Run a thin-bladed knife around the inside of each mold to loosen the timbales before unmolding. Invert the timbales onto eight individual serving plates, and remove the molds and the wax paper. **2.** Pour about 2 tablespoons of the Chardonnay Butter Sauce onto each plate. Garnish with the roasted red pepper cutouts.

FETTUCCINE WITH MOREL MUSHROOMS AND COUNTRY HAM

Every spring, if we get exactly the right amount of light rain followed by just enough sunshine, we're blessed with a bountiful harvest of wild morels, which the local mountain people refer to as "merkels." Some say the name is of German derivation (the Teutonic word for morel was merchel). Others insist that merkel is Southern for miracle.

At any rate, the arrival of the first merkel of the season is greeted with as much excitement as any miracle would be. A buzz goes from hollow to hollow about who found it, where it was found, and how big it was. Predictions are made about how good the season will be, and tall tales are exchanged about previous harvests. The almost otherworldly aspect of merkel hunting is that not everybody is capable of seeing the mushroom's distinctive cap poking up in the forest. You have to have a trained eye.

No other mushroom has a richer, earthier, or meatier taste than the morel. In this dish, the flavor permeates the cream. You may substitute dried morels (after soaking them in warm water for a few minutes) or try other varieties of mushrooms, such as chanterelles.

SERVES 4

1. Bring 4 quarts of water to a rolling boil and add the salt. Cook the fettuccine until just barely al dente. Drain in a colander and toss with 1 tablespoon of the oil. Keep warm. **2.** In a 10-inch sauté pan, melt the butter and the remaining 1 tablespoon oil over high heat. Add the morels just as the butter begins to color. Sauté rapidly until the mushrooms begin to crisp around the edges. Add the shallot and garlic and sauté for 1 minute more. Remove from the heat. **3.** In a 4-quart saucepan, bring the cream to a boil. Reduce the heat and add half of the sautéed mushrooms. Reserve the other half for garnish. Cook until the cream thickens enough to coat the back of a spoon. Stir in the cheese. Add the nutmeg and season with salt and pepper. **4.** Add the fettuccine to the sauce and toss well to combine.

TO SERVE: Using tongs, place a mound of fettuccine in each of four warm serving bowls and pour a bit of the remaining sauce over the noodles. Place the reserved mushrooms on top of the fettuccine and divide the ham evenly among the bowls. Garnish with the chives.

1 teaspoon salt

8 ounces fresh fettuccine or 4 ounces dried

2 tablespoons olive oil

1 tablespoon butter

1 cup fresh morel mushrooms or ¼ cup dried reconstituted in warm water

½ teaspoon minced shallot

¼ teaspoon minced garlic

3 cups heavy cream

½ cup freshly grated Parmesan cheese

Pinch of freshly ground nutmeg

Salt and freshly ground pepper to taste

2 very thin slices well-trimmed country ham, cut into ribbons the same width as the fettuccine

1 tablespoon chopped fresh chives

*Black-Eyed Peas Vinaigrette
(recipe follows)*

*1 cup delicate mixed greens, such as
frisée, mâche (corn salad), watercress, or
red oak lettuce, washed and well drained*

1 tablespoon extra-virgin olive oil

*4 small, very thin slices cooked
country ham*

*4 slices fresh American foie gras, about
½ inch thick and 1½ ounces each*

Salt and freshly ground pepper to taste

1 teaspoon finely chopped shallot

½ teaspoon minced garlic

½ cup balsamic vinegar

1 tablespoon finely chopped scallions

AMERICAN FOIE GRAS SAUTÉ WITH BLACK-EYED PEAS VINAIGRETTE

*This dish is simply a seared slice of warm fattened duck liver resting on a salad
of black-eyed peas and little greens. A slice of country ham strengthens the
Southern accent, and a hot, vinegary reduction of the pan juices becomes the
sauce. See Crispy Seared Foie Gras on Polenta with Country Ham and
Blackberries (page 20) for notes on foie gras.*

SERVES 4

1. Place about ¼ cup of the Black-Eyed Peas Vinaigrette in the center of each of four serving plates.   **2.** In a small bowl, combine the mixed greens with the oil and toss lightly. Arrange the greens around the peas and place a slice of ham on top.   **3.** Sprinkle the foie gras with salt and pepper. Place a medium-size sauté pan or skillet over high heat. Add the foie gras and brown on both sides, about 30 seconds per side. Place on top of the ham.   **4.** Remove half of the fat from the pan, then add the shallot, garlic, and vinegar. Cook, stirring constantly, until the sauce is reduced by one-half.

TO SERVE: Spoon equal amounts of sauce over each serving of foie gras. Sprinkle with the scallions and serve immediately.

38

BLACK-EYED PEAS VINAIGRETTE

In the restaurant's early years, our entire kitchen staff consisted of several very Southern women. On New Year's Day, they would insist on cooking black-eyed peas for our "family" meal. They convinced me that it was absolutely essential to eat them for good luck.

One year my peas got cold, so I sprinkled a little salad dressing on them and thought they tasted better that way. Foie gras (fattened duck liver) had just become available in America, and I was constantly trying new ways of preparing it. Combining this expensive delicacy with traditional Southern slave food created an interesting balance. American Foie Gras Sauté with Black-Eyed Peas Vinaigrette was born.

It wasn't long before Craig Claibourne visited, tried the dish, and wrote that it was one of the best things he had ever tasted. The recipe appeared in The New York Times *and the dish became a sort of symbolic illustration of what was to become the New American Cuisine—unlikely combinations artistically presented in new and refined ways—in essence, the emerging of an American haute cuisine.*

These peas are also wonderful with baked ham on a buffet table or at a picnic. They taste best at room temperature.

Makes 1 cup

1. Rinse the peas in a colander under cold running water. Place them in a 2-quart saucepan, cover with cold water, and soak overnight. (Or bring the water to a boil, cook for 1 minute, remove from the heat, cover, and let soak for 1 hour.)   2. Drain the peas.   3. Place the ham or goose skin and fat, bay leaves, onion, garlic, parsley, thyme, and peppercorns in a 10-inch square of cheesecloth and tie into a pouch using kitchen string.   4. In a large saucepan, combine the peas, water, and vinegar. Add the cheesecloth bag and bring to a boil. Simmer for 15 to 20 minutes, or until the peas are tender but not mushy.   5. Drain the peas, discarding the cheesecloth bag, and pour the Tarragon Vinaigrette over them while they are still hot. Let the peas come to room temperature and season with salt and pepper.

N O T E :   You can make this recipe several days in advance and keep refrigerated.

¼ pound dried black-eyed peas
¼ pound skin and fat from smoked ham or smoked goose breast
4 bay leaves
⅓ cup finely chopped onion
2 large cloves garlic, peeled
6 sprigs fresh parsley
3 sprigs fresh thyme or ½ teaspoon dried
1 teaspoon crushed black peppercorns
3 cups water
2 tablespoons balsamic vinegar
¼ cup Tarragon Vinaigrette (see page 166)
Salt and freshly ground pepper to taste

3

SOUPS

¼ cup (½ stick) lightly salted butter

1 medium-size onion, coarsely chopped

2 leeks, chopped

2 stalks celery, coarsely chopped

*3 medium-size Idaho potatoes,
peeled and coarsely chopped*

2 bay leaves, crumbled

*2 quarts chicken stock, preferably
homemade (see page 170)*

2 pounds fresh asparagus

3 tablespoons olive oil

1½ cups heavy cream

Salt and freshly ground pepper to taste

Lemon Cream (recipe follows)

PUREE OF FRESH ASPARAGUS SOUP WITH LEMON CREAM

All winter long, we dream about the first fresh asparagus from our neighbor's garden. When the season is finally upon us, we can't resist buying all that comes our way. We use the tips in a variety of dishes and often are left with an abundance of stalks. This soup is the perfect solution to that problem. It can be made in advance and freezes well. A dollop of chilled Lemon Cream adds a dressy and refreshing note to the soup.

SERVES 6

1. In a 4-quart heavy-bottomed saucepan, melt the butter over medium heat. Add the onion, leeks, and celery and cook until tender but not browned. 2. Add the potatoes and bay leaves. Cook for 5 minutes. 3. Meanwhile, in a separate saucepan, bring the stock to a boil. Add the boiling stock to the vegetables and simmer until the potatoes are soft, about 15 to 20 minutes. 4. While the soup is simmering, remove and discard any tough white ends from the asparagus. Wash the stalks, and cut into 1-inch pieces. 5. In a 10-inch skillet, sauté pan, or wok, heat the oil over very high heat. Sauté the asparagus in three batches, cooking only until it turns a brilliant green but is still very firm. Reserve the cooked asparagus in a bowl, then add it to the simmering soup all at once. 6. Cook the soup about 4 minutes, or until the asparagus is just barely tender but still bright green. 7. Remove the soup from the heat and puree in small batches in a blender or food processor. 8. Strain the soup. Add the cream and return to the heat. Season with salt and pepper.

TO SERVE: Serve the soup in individual bowls with a dollop of Lemon Cream.

NOTE: Asparagus should be stored as you would fresh flowers, standing upright in a little water or on moist paper towels in the refrigerator.

½ cup heavy cream

1 tablespoon fresh lemon juice

1 teaspoon grated lemon zest

Pinch of sugar

LEMON CREAM

MAKES 1 CUP

In the bowl of an electric mixer, combine the cream, lemon juice and zest, and sugar. Whip until stiff peaks form.

Our Garden Sorrel Vichyssoise

French sorrel is a leafy, intensely flavored, lemony herb that is surprisingly easy to grow but not easy to find in most supermarkets. Fortunately, watercress makes a very agreeable substitute and is readily available year-round. Spinach may also be used, but it imparts less flavor.

This soup is a beautiful sea-foam green and fabulously refreshing. If you're concerned with calories, you can reduce the amount of cream or serve just a demitasse of the soup, as we do at The Inn.

Serves 6

1. In a 4-quart heavy-bottomed saucepan, melt the butter over medium heat. Add the onion and leeks and cook until tender but not browned, about 7 minutes. 2. Add the potato and bay leaves and cook for 5 minutes. 3. Meanwhile, in a separate saucepan, heat the stock to a boil. Pour the boiling stock over the vegetables. Simmer until the potato is soft, about 15 minutes. 4. Remove the soup from the heat and puree in small batches in a blender or food processor. Strain. Chill in the refrigerator. 5. When the soup is thoroughly chilled, add the sorrel and puree again in a blender or food processor. 6. Transfer the soup to a bowl and whisk in the lemon juice and vinegar. Add the cream. Season with salt and white pepper. Chill thoroughly in the refrigerator.

To serve: Pour the chilled soup into bowls and sprinkle with the chives.

Note: When heated, sorrel leaves tend to lose their delicate green color and turn a rather unappealing army green. Be sure the soup is well chilled before incorporating them.

¼ cup (½ stick) lightly salted butter

1 medium-size onion, coarsely chopped

3 leeks, chopped

3 medium-size Idaho potatoes, peeled and diced

2 bay leaves

2 quarts chicken stock, preferably homemade (see page 170)

1 cup fresh sorrel leaves, stemmed and chopped

1 tablespoon fresh lemon juice

⅛ cup red wine vinegar

2 cups heavy cream

Salt and white pepper to taste

2 tablespoons chopped fresh chives

½ cup olive oil

1 cup chopped onion

1 tablespoon dried fennel seed

¼ teaspoon dried thyme

½ bay leaf, crumbled

½ teaspoon minced garlic

1 tablespoon chopped fresh basil or
½ teaspoon dried

2 tablespoons minced jalapeño pepper

¼ cup all-purpose flour

5 cups chicken stock, preferably
homemade (see page 170)

½ cup peeled, seeded, and chopped fresh
or canned tomato

1 teaspoon tomato paste

6 large red bell peppers, halved, seeded,
and cut into 2-inch chunks

½ to 1 cup heavy cream

Pinch of sugar

Salt and freshly ground pepper to taste

Generous splash of sambuca

Sambuca Cream (recipe follows)

Sweet Red Bell Pepper Soup with Sambuca Cream

This relatively simple, full-flavored soup is the hands-down favorite of our guests year after year. Its complex, subtle heat manages to titillate everybody's palate. The Sambuca Cream garnish takes just seconds to whip up and, like the soup, can be made well in advance.

Serves 6

1. In a 4-quart heavy-bottomed saucepan, heat the ½ cup oil over medium heat. Add the onion, fennel seed, thyme, bay leaf, garlic, basil, and jalapeño pepper. Reduce the heat to low and cook until the onion is translucent, about 10 to 15 minutes. 2. Add the flour and cook, stirring constantly, for 10 minutes. 3. In a separate pot, bring the stock to a boil. Carefully pour the stock over the vegetables, stirring well to incorporate. Add the tomato and tomato paste. 4. Meanwhile, place a large skillet lightly coated with olive oil over high heat. Sauté the bell pepper chunks until the skins are blistered and lightly charred. Add the peppers to the soup and simmer, stirring occasionally to make sure nothing sticks to the bottom of the pot, for about 20 minutes. 5. Remove the soup from the heat and puree in small batches in a blender or food processor fitted with a steel blade. Strain. 6. Return the soup to the saucepan, bring to a simmer, and add ½ cup of the cream and the sugar. Season with salt and pepper. If the soup is too spicy, add more cream. Add the sambuca just before serving.

To serve: Serve the soup in individual bowls with a dollop of Sambuca Cream.

Note: The soup can be made up to 2 days in advance and slowly reheated. Don't add the sambuca until you are ready to serve.

1 cup heavy cream

½ teaspoon fresh lemon juice

¼ teaspoon grated lemon zest

3 tablespoons sambuca

Pinch of sugar

Sambuca Cream

Makes 1 cup

In the bowl of an electric mixer, whip the cream until soft peaks form. Add the lemon juice and zest, sambuca, and sugar. Continue whipping until the cream is almost stiff. Keep refrigerated until serving time.

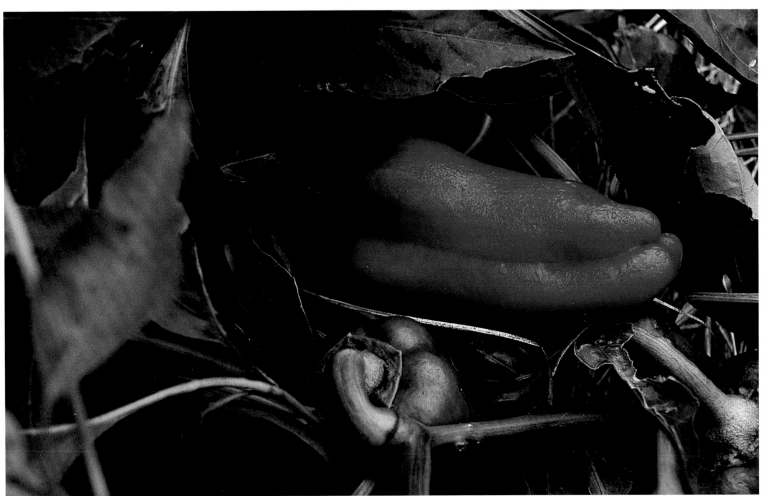

3½ pounds fresh yellow tomatoes, cored and coarsely chopped

½ cucumber, peeled, seeded, and coarsely chopped

1 yellow bell pepper, seeded and chopped

½ jalapeño pepper, sliced lengthwise, seeded, and chopped

½ Vidalia onion, coarsely chopped

2 stalks celery, coarsely chopped

½ teaspoon minced garlic

3 tablespoons extra-virgin olive oil

½ teaspoon Tabasco

1 tablespoon fresh lemon juice

1 tablespoon rice wine vinegar

1 teaspoon sugar

½ teaspoon ground cumin

½ teaspoon celery salt

Salt and freshly ground pepper to taste

GARNISHES

2 tablespoons seeded and minced red bell pepper

2 tablespoons seeded and minced green bell pepper

2 tablespoons peeled, seeded, and minced cucumber

2 tablespoons minced red onion

2 tablespoons chopped fresh chives

⅓ cup croutons

2 bottles (750 ml each) Virginia Riesling

8 whole cloves

1 cinnamon stick

2 bay leaves

¼ cup firmly packed brown sugar

12 peaches, peeled and stoned

1 orange, sliced

1 lemon, sliced

1½ cups heavy cream

Splash of fresh lemon juice

GOLDEN GAZPACHO

This version of the traditional spicy, chilled Spanish soup calls for yellow tomatoes (which are lower in acidity than red ones) and can be used as a sauce for steamed lobster, as shown on the opposite page. If you don't have access to yellow tomatoes, red ones will work just fine.

SERVES 6

1. In a blender or food processor fitted with a steel blade, puree the tomato, cucumber, bell pepper, jalapeño pepper, onion, and celery. Add the garlic. Strain and refrigerate. **2.** When the puree is thoroughly chilled, add the oil, Tabasco, lemon juice, vinegar, and sugar. Mix well. Add the cumin, celery salt, and salt and pepper. Refrigerate.

TO SERVE: Serve well chilled with any or all of the garnishes.

CHILLED PEACH SOUP WITH VIRGINIA RIESLING

Here's a marvelously refreshing hot-weather soup to make when you have an abundance of peaches on hand. Bruised or overripe fruit works just fine. The soup can be made several days in advance, refrigerated, and creamed just before serving. Garnish with toasted almonds or blackberry puree for an added touch. If you can't find Virginia Riesling, California or Alsatian will do.

SERVES 6

1. In a 6-quart heavy-bottomed saucepan, combine the Riesling, cloves, cinnamon stick, bay leaves, and brown sugar. Bring to a rapid boil. Add the peaches, reduce the heat, and let simmer for 20 to 25 minutes. **2.** Add the orange and lemon slices. Continue cooking for 5 minutes. **3.** Remove the cloves, cinnamon stick, bay leaf, and orange and lemon slices from the soup. Puree the soup in small batches in a blender or food processor. Strain. Chill in the refrigerator. **4.** When the soup is chilled, add the cream and lemon juice.

¼ cup (½ stick) butter

1 medium onion, coarsely chopped

½ leek, cut into 1-inch pieces

2 stalks celery, chopped

1 bay leaf

1 medium Idaho potato,
peeled and chopped

1 medium celery root, peeled and chopped

1 quart chicken stock, preferably
homemade (see page 170)

½ cinnamon stick

½ cup heavy cream

Salt, white pepper, sugar, and freshly
grated nutmeg to taste

24 pale green celery leaves

CELERY AND CELERY ROOT BISQUE

*We serve this elegant and unusual soup in the fall and winter. The combination of
fresh celery and celery root bring about a double depth of subtle flavors.*

SERVES 6

1. In a 4-quart saucepan, melt the butter over low heat. Add the onion, leek, and celery. Cook until the vegetables are tender, about 10 minutes.   **2.** Add the bay leaf, potato, and celery root and cook for 5 minutes.   **3.** Meanwhile, in a separate saucepan, heat the stock to a simmer.   **4.** Add the heated stock to the vegetables and bring to a boil over medium heat. Immediately reduce the heat to low and add the cinnamon stick. Simmer until the celery root is soft.   **5.** Remove the cinnamon stick from the soup. Puree the soup in small batches in a blender or food processor. Strain, pressing hard on the solids to force as much of the vegetable mixture through the strainer as possible.   **6.** Pour the strained soup into a clean saucepan and return to the stove over low heat. Add the cream and season with salt, white pepper, sugar, and nutmeg.

TO SERVE: Pour the soup into individual bowls and garnish with the celery leaves.

3 tablespoons butter

1 medium-size onion, coarsely chopped

9 cups chicken stock, preferably
homemade (see page 170)

1 teaspoon curry powder

5 to 6 medium-size sweet potatoes,
peeled and cubed

¼ cup maple syrup

2 to 3 sprigs fresh thyme or
1 teaspoon dried

Pinch of cayenne pepper

1 cup cream

⅛ teaspoon freshly grated nutmeg

Salt and white pepper to taste

Rum Cream (recipe follows)

SWEET POTATO SOUP WITH RUM CREAM

*This is an elegant, surprisingly simple and inexpensive soup to make
during the winter holidays. We serve it on Thanksgiving.*

SERVES 10

1. In a 6-quart heavy-bottomed saucepan, melt the butter over medium heat. Add the onion and curry powder and cook for about 6 minutes, stirring occasionally.   **2.** Meanwhile, in a separate saucepan, heat the stock to a simmer.   **3.** Add the sweet potato to the onion, then add the heated stock, maple syrup, thyme, and cayenne. Cook until the sweet potato is soft, about 25 minutes.   **4.** Remove the thyme sprigs from the soup, puree the soup in small batches, and strain.   **5.** Return the soup to the heat and add the cream, nutmeg, and salt and white pepper.

TO SERVE: Transfer the soup to individual bowls and serve with a dollop of Rum Cream.

1 cup heavy cream

½ teaspoon fresh lemon juice

¼ teaspoon grated lemon zest

3 tablespoons good-quality dark rum

Pinch of sugar

RUM CREAM

MAKES 2 CUPS

In the bowl of an electric mixer, whip the cream until soft peaks form. Add the lemon juice and zest, rum, and sugar. Continue whipping until the cream is almost stiff. Refrigerate until ready to serve.

½ cup dried black beans

3 strips bacon, chopped, or
¼-pound smoked ham hock

1 cup chopped onion

½ cup chopped green bell pepper

½ cup chopped leeks

½ cup chopped carrot

½ cup chopped celery

1 quart chicken stock, preferably
homemade (see page 170)

5 bay leaves

1 teaspoon chopped fresh thyme
or 1 teaspoon dried

2 cloves garlic, crushed

1 ham bone (optional)

1 teaspoon dry mustard

Salt and cayenne pepper to taste

½ cup sherry

OPTIONAL GARNISHES

Chopped hard-boiled egg

Diced red onion

Diced red and green bell pepper

Crème fraîche

Crisp fried tortilla crisps

½ pound dried cannellini or
Great Northern beans

5 strips bacon, diced

2 medium-size onions, coarsely chopped

3 leeks, chopped

1 cup chopped celery

4 bay leaves

4 quarts chicken stock, preferably
homemade (see page 170)

1 ham bone (optional)

2 cups heavy cream

Salt and cayenne pepper to taste

BLACK BEAN SOUP

Nothing is heartier or more warming on a cold winter day than this full-flavored soup, tinged with the subtle smoky flavor of an old ham bone and accompanied by a glass of dry sherry. It's enough to make you look forward to inclement weather. Dressed up with all the optional garnishes it becomes a luncheon main course needing only a composed salad to round out the menu. For a simple but hearty family meal, it can be served over steamed white rice. It's always a good idea to make a large amount and freeze quart-size containers to have on hand for snow days.

SERVES 6

1. In a medium-size pan, cover the beans with cold water and soak overnight. 2. The next morning, rinse the beans, drain, and set aside. 3. In an 8-quart heavy-bottomed stockpot, cook the bacon or ham hock over medium heat until browned. Add the onion, pepper, leeks, carrot, and celery. Continue cooking until the vegetables are tender, about 15 minutes. 4. Meanwhile, in a separate saucepan, heat the stock. 5. Add the beans, bay leaves, thyme, and garlic to the vegetables. Add the heated stock and ham bone (if using). Simmer until the beans are very tender, about 1 hour. 6. Remove the ham bone and ham hock (if using) from the soup. Puree the soup in small batches in a blender or food processor. Strain. 7. Return the soup to the heat, add the mustard, and season with salt and cayenne. Add the sherry just before serving and pass the optional garnishes on the side.

PUREE OF WHITE BEAN SOUP

This is the world's most refined version of bean soup. Pureeing the beans and adding a touch of cream makes for a delicate soup, but all the hearty flavors remain intact — the best of both worlds, and a perfect beginning for a fall or cold weather dinner. For an interesting presentation, try serving the white bean and black bean soups together in the same bowl. Simply have a pitcher of each and pour half white and half black into each soup bowl, letting your guests swirl them together.

SERVES 8

1. In a medium-size saucepan, cover the beans with cool water and soak overnight. 2. In an 8-quart heavy-bottomed stockpot, cook the bacon over medium heat until browned. Add the onion, leeks, celery, and bay leaves and cook until the vegetables are tender, about 15 minutes. 3. Meanwhile, in a separate saucepan, heat the stock to boiling. 4. Rinse and drain the beans and add them to the stockpot along with the heated stock and ham bone (if using). Simmer until the beans are very soft, about 1 hour. 5. Remove the ham bone from the soup. Puree the soup in small batches in a blender or food processor and strain. 6. Return the soup to the heat and add the cream. If the soup is too thick, add more stock or cream. Season with salt and cayenne.

4

SALADS

Ingredients

2 large fresh beets

½ cup heavy cream

2 tablespoons red wine vinegar

Salt and white pepper to taste

36 large spears asparagus

2 cups vegetable oil

6 quail eggs

*1 cup Tarragon Vinaigrette
(see page 166)*

3 tablespoons capers, drained

¼ cup pistachio nuts, toasted

*2 tablespoons coarsely chopped
fresh parsley*

Coarsely cracked black pepper

1 tablespoon extra-virgin olive oil

ASPARAGUS SALAD WITH PICKLED QUAIL EGGS AND BEET VINAIGRETTE

The gorgeous colors of this salad seem to shout "Spring!" You don't have to use quail eggs—regular chicken eggs will do fine, although they'll need a longer time to soak up the red color of the beet juice. Only the freshest asparagus—never frozen—should be used. While the recipe might sound complicated, it's merely an assemblage of individual components that can be readied well in advance.

SERVES 6

1. Place the beets in a saucepan with enough water to cover. Bring to a boil, reduce to a simmer, and cook until tender, about 15 to 20 minutes. Allow the beets to cool to room temperature in their cooking liquid. **2.** Remove the beets from the pan, reserving the liquid. Peel the beets, then use the smallest melon ball scoop (½ inch or less in diameter) to make about 18 beet balls for garnish. **3.** Coarsely chop the remaining beet scraps and puree in a blender, using the reserved beet cooking liquid to create a very smooth puree. **4.** In the bowl of an electric mixer, beat the cream until soft peaks form. Fold in ½ cup of the beet puree and 1 tablespoon of the red wine vinegar until thoroughly incorporated. Season with salt and white pepper. Chill in the refrigerator. **5.** Bring a large pot of salted water to a rolling boil. Fill a large bowl with ice water. Trim the ends of 30 of the asparagus spears evenly and peel if necessary. Drop the asparagus into the boiling water and cook, uncovered, until tender, about 6 to 7 minutes. Remove the spears and immediately refresh in ice water until well chilled. Drain thoroughly. **6.** With a vegetable peeler, slice the remaining 6 asparagus spears into long, thin ribbons. In a 2-quart saucepan, heat the vegetable oil to 375 degrees, or until a 1-inch cube of bread browns in 1 minute. In several batches, deep-fry the asparagus ribbons in the hot oil until golden brown. Remove with a strainer or slotted spoon and drain on paper towels. Lightly season with salt. **7.** In a small saucepan, cover the eggs with cold water. Bring to a boil, remove the eggs, and immediately place in ice water for several minutes to stop the cooking. Peel the eggs and place them in a bowl with enough reserved beet cooking liquid to cover. Add the remaining 1 tablespoon red wine vinegar. Allow the eggs to rest in the liquid for 5 minutes. **8.** In a large bowl, toss the cooked asparagus spears with the Tarragon Vinaigrette until evenly coated. Add 1 tablespoon of the capers. Toss again with salt and white pepper.

TO SERVE: **1.** On each of six chilled dinner plates, lay out five spears of dressed asparagus in a neat bundle. Toss the beet balls, pistachios, parsley, remaining 2 tablespoons capers, and cracked black pepper in a swath across each plate. In the center of each asparagus bundle, place a dollop of the chilled creamy beet dressing. **2.** Cut the pickled eggs in half lengthwise and place one half on each side of the bundle, next to the dressing. Mound the fried asparagus ribbons on top. Drizzle a little olive oil on each plate.

¾ cup extra-virgin olive oil

¼ cup balsamic vinegar

1 teaspoon ground cinnamon

¼ teaspoon ground nutmeg

1 large red onion

4 navel oranges

1 bunch watercress

ORANGE-ONION SALAD

This is a Moroccan twist on an old Italian combination. It makes for a pretty addition to a buffet table or lends an exotic note under roast chicken.

SERVES 4

1. Preheat the grill or broiler.   2. In a small bowl, combine the oil, vinegar, cinnamon, and nutmeg.   3. Slice the onion about ⅛ inch thick and toss in the marinade.   4. Lay the onion slices in a single layer on the grill rack or spread out on a baking sheet and place under the broiler. Cook on both sides, turning with tongs, until wilted. Remove from the heat and set aside.   5. Peel the oranges with a sharp, flexible knife, carefully removing all the white membrane. Slice about ¼ inch thick, remove any seeds, and lay the slices in a shallow pan. Pour the marinade over them.

TO SERVE: Place about four slices of the marinated orange slices on each of four salad plates in the shape of a four-leaf clover. Scatter the grilled onions on top of the oranges. Garnish with sprigs of watercress. Serve at room temperature.

CHILLED BEET PASTA SALAD WITH STOLICHNAYA VINAIGRETTE AND OSSETRA CAVIAR

Wouldn't you guess we created this shocking crimson-colored pasta dish for an all-red menu on Valentine's Day? The fabulous color and intense beet taste of the fettuccine is achieved by the simple trick of cooking beet pasta in boiling beet juice. You simply save the red beet liquid you've cooked the beets in and use it again to boil the pasta. If you don't want to bother with making your own pasta, don't. Just buy any good-quality fettuccine and cook the noodles in beet juice. If you don't want to bother using fresh beets just get a can of beets packed in water and drain the juice and add it to your pasta cooking water.

This salad lends itself to any variety of garnishes or additions. Caviar is certainly one of the most festive accompaniments and goes beautifully with the vodka vinaigrette.

SERVES 6

TO MAKE THE PASTA: **1.** In a food processor fitted with a steel blade, combine the flour, salt, and oil until incorporated. Add the egg and beet puree and process until the dough is smooth and evenly colored. Let rest for 1 hour in the refrigerator. **2.** Cut the chilled dough into four equal pieces and roll out on a pasta machine through the widest setting about six times. Reduce the setting and roll out six times more, each time reducing the setting. Let the pasta dry for about 5 minutes and roll through the pasta machine on the fettuccine cutter. Hang the fettuccine over a dowel or broomstick to dry for about 5 minutes. (The pasta may be dusted with flour and stored in the refrigerator for up to 2 days.) **3.** In a large pot, bring 3 quarts beet cooking liquid or 1½ quarts beet juice and 1½ quarts water to a rolling boil. Drop the pasta into the boiling liquid and cook for about 3 minutes. **4.** Drain the pasta in a colander, discarding the beet liquid, and plunge into ice water for 1 minute to stop the cooking. **5.** Drain thoroughly before dressing.

TO MAKE THE VINAIGRETTE: In a small bowl, whisk together the oil, lemon juice and zest, vodka, and salt and pepper. (The dressing may be made several days in advance and stored in the refrigerator.)

TO SERVE: **1.** Toss the pasta with the vinaigrette, using only enough liquid to coat and thoroughly moisten the noodles. Adjust the seasonings. **2.** Using a large fork, twirl the pasta into coils and place a coiled mound in each of six flat soup plates. Place a dollop of crème fraîche on each mound and top with one-sixth of the caviar. Sprinkle with the egg and about ½ teaspoon each of the capers, onion, and chives. **3.** Grind some pepper on the rim of the bowl and serve immediately.

BEET PASTA
2½ cups all-purpose flour
1 teaspoon salt
1 tablespoon olive oil
1 egg
¼ cup beet puree (be sure to save the cooking water if you are making your own puree)

STOLICHNAYA VODKA VINAIGRETTE
½ cup extra-virgin olive oil
¼ cup fresh lemon juice
Grated zest of 1 lemon
¼ cup Stolichnaya or other good-quality vodka
Salt and freshly ground pepper to taste

GARNISHES
2 tablespoons crème fraîche
3 ounces fresh Ossetra caviar
1 hard-boiled egg, finely chopped
1 tablespoon capers, drained
1 tablespoon minced red onion
1 tablespoon chopped fresh chives
Freshly ground pepper

½ cup red wine vinegar

6 sprigs fresh basil

½ cup pine nuts

1 bunch watercress

4 ripe garden tomatoes

2 red onions

Salt and cracked black pepper to taste

¼ cup plus extra-virgin olive oil

One 8-ounce wedge Asiago cheese

½ cup vinaigrette

Sugar to taste

Fresh basil leaves

GARDEN TOMATO SALAD WITH GRILLED RED ONIONS, FRESH BASIL, AND ASIAGO CHEESE

We look forward to this wonderfully simple tomato salad all winter long and can't get enough of it during tomato season. Phyllis Richman, restaurant reviewer for The Washington Post, *has called it "the best tomato salad in the world." It should really only be made when beautifully ripe garden tomatoes are available.*

SERVES 4 TO 6

1. In a small saucepan, bring the vinegar and basil sprigs to a simmer. Remove from the heat and steep until cool. Strain and reserve. (This may be done well in advance and stored in the refrigerator.)   2. Preheat the oven to 350 degrees.   3. Spread the pine nuts in a single layer on a baking sheet and toast until golden brown, about 5 minutes. Check frequently to avoid burning.   4. Trim the watercress, discarding any wilted leaves and cutting off all but about 1½ inches of the stems.   5. Cut the tomatoes into ¼-inch-thick slices.   6. Cut the onions into ⅛-inch-thick slices and season with salt and cracked black pepper. Toss with the ¼ cup oil and grill over medium heat until lightly charred and wilted.   7. With a vegetable peeler, slice the cheese into ribbonlike curls and set aside.

TO SERVE: 1. Chill six plates.   2. Toss the watercress with the vinaigrette and make a nest of it on each plate.   3. Arrange three large slices of tomato on top of the watercress in a circular pattern. Lightly sprinkle with salt, pepper, and sugar, then spoon a little of the basil-flavored red wine vinegar on top.   4. Place several rings of the grilled onions on top of the tomatoes and sprinkle with the toasted pine nuts. Arrange three ribbons of cheese on top of each salad. Drizzle with extra-virgin olive oil and garnish with a few basil leaves.

5

MAIN DISHES

6 whole poussins, about 1¼ pounds each

MARINADE
1 pint fresh blackberries or blueberries
⅔ cup red wine vinegar
¼ cup olive oil
1 bay leaf
¼ teaspoon dried thyme
Pinch of minced garlic

GARNISH AND SAUCE
2 tablespoons unsalted butter
½ pint fresh blackberries or blueberries
¼ cup chicken stock, preferably
homemade (see page 170)
1 cup crème fraîche or sour cream
1 tablespoon chopped fresh chives

CHARCOAL-GRILLED POUSSINS MARINATED IN BLACKBERRY VINEGAR

We always refer to this dish as "blue chicken" because the marinade turns the flesh of the tiny chickens (poussins) an intriguing inky blue color, while the vinegar tenderizes the meat. Because the poussins are boned, they are able to lie completely flat and cook very quickly over the fire. The skin crisps and burns easily, so we usually grill them briefly on both sides to capture the smoky charcoal flavor and then finish cooking them in the oven.

This dish makes a wonderful main course for an informal outdoor supper, or the birds can be dressed up and presented individually on a potato cake with a dollop of crème fraîche and warmed berries strewn over them. Blackberries and blueberries work equally well in the marinade. You can substitute boned quail or cornish game hens for the poussins.

SERVES 6

1. In a 2-quart saucepan, combine 1 pint of the berries and the vinegar over medium heat and bring just to a boil. Remove from the heat and let stand for 1 hour at room temperature. Strain, discarding the solids. **2.** In a shallow nonreactive pan big enough to hold the poussins, combine the strained vinegar mixture, oil, bay leaf, thyme, and garlic. Set aside. **3.** Lay each poussin breast side down on a cutting board and, using poultry shears, snip off the wing tips at the second joint. Next, cut out the entire backbone, spreading the chicken flat. With a sharp boning knife, make an incision along the center of the breastbone. Remove the breastbone with your fingers. Gently lift the rib bones from the breast meat by running the knife underneath the bones. Continue in this manner, removing all the bones except the first joint of the leg and the wing. **4.** Place the boned birds in the marinade, turning to coat evenly. Let stand at room temperature for 2 hours, or cover and refrigerate overnight. **5.** Prepare a charcoal fire, letting the flames subside to glowing embers. Lay the birds skin side down on the grill rack. Cook for about 3 minutes, allowing the skin to crisp but not burn. Using tongs, turn the birds over and cook for about 3 minutes more. (The poussins may be prepared to this point up to 1 hour prior to serving.) **6.** Preheat the oven to 400 degrees. **7.** Place the birds on a baking sheet and bake for about 8 minutes, or until the juices run clear when the flesh is pierced with a knife.

TO SERVE: 1. Put the poussins on a platter or six individual plates. **2.** Place an 8-inch sauté pan over high heat. Add the butter and remaining ½ pint berries. Coat the berries evenly with the butter and deglaze the pan with the stock. Continue cooking until sauce coats the back of a spoon. **3.** Spoon the berries and sauce over the birds or pass in a sauceboat. Finish with a dollop of crème fraîche or sour cream and a sprinkling of chives on each poussin.

4 poussins, about 1 pound each
Salt and freshly ground pepper to taste
Vegetable oil

SAUCE

3 tablespoons olive oil
⅓ cup chopped onion
⅓ cup chopped carrot
⅓ cup chopped celery
1 bay leaf
1 teaspoon chopped fresh thyme or
½ teaspoon dried
1½ quarts chicken stock, preferably
homemade (see page 170)

Orange-Onion Salad (see page 60)
Wild Rice Pecan Pilaf (see page 115)

ROAST POUSSINS WITH ORANGE-ONION SALAD

This is simply a little roast chicken placed on a bed of Moroccan-inspired Orange-Onion Salad. The poussin is boned and sliced except for the drumsticks and wing tips and reassembled over a mound of Wild Rice Pecan Pilaf. The combination of flavors is exotic and refreshing—perfect for a light summer dinner or luncheon. The sauce may be omitted if you're short on time. The dish will be just as wonderful if you use a larger roasting chicken or cornish game hens instead of the poussins.

SERVES 4

TO MAKE THE SAUCE: **1.** In a 4-quart heavy-bottomed saucepan set over medium heat, combine the oil, onion, carrot, and celery. Stir occasionally, letting the vegetables begin to brown. **2.** Add the bay leaf and thyme. Add the chicken stock and simmer for about 45 minutes. **3.** Strain the sauce, put it back in the pan, and reduce it over high heat for about 10 minutes, or until flavors are concentrated. (Sauce will have a brothlike consistency.) Check the seasoning. Keep warm.

TO COOK THE POUSSINS: **1.** Preheat the oven to 400 degrees. **2.** Season the birds with salt and pepper. **3.** Place a large sauté pan over medium-high heat and add oil to a depth of 1 inch. When the oil is very hot, carefully lay the poussins breast side down in the pan and sauté until golden brown on all sides, using tongs to turn the birds. **4.** Drain the oil from the pan and place the poussins in the oven. Roast for about 10 minutes, or until the juices run clear when the leg meat is pierced with a fork. Remove from the oven and keep warm.

TO SERVE: **1.** Arrange four portions of the Orange-Onion Salad (omitting the watercress) on four warm plates. Place a mound of warm Wild Rice Pecan Pilaf in the center of the salad. **2.** Using a sharp, flexible knife, remove the legs and thighs from the poussins. Then, running the knife against the bone, slip the breast meat off in one piece. Remove all the bones except the leg bones. Slice each breast into four pieces and reassemble the birds on top of the rice. **3.** Ladle the warm sauce onto the plate and serve immediately.

CALVES' LIVER SAUTÉ WITH ORANGES AND ONION CONFITURE

On one of my first trips to France, I tasted a caramelized onion "marmalade" in Lyon, the onion capital of the world, and loved it. I thought it would make the perfect component for an elegant version of liver and onions.

Orange sections sprinkled with shreds of candied orange zest make a refreshing garnish for this crisp, tender liver along with a mound of caramelized onions. The liver is sauced with a quick reduction of the pan juices, white wine, chicken stock, orange juice, and cream.

SERVES 4

TO MAKE THE ONION CONFITURE: 1. Peel and slice the onions as thinly as possible. 2. In a large, heavy-bottomed sauté pan over medium heat, melt the butter and add the sliced onions, stirring with a wooden spoon until wilted. Reduce the heat and continue cooking, stirring occasionally, until the onions begin to turn a light golden color, about 30 minutes. 3. Sprinkle the onions with the sugar and continue cooking, stirring often, until the color deepens to a rich nut brown. 4. Add the orange juice and remove from the heat. You should have about 2 cups of confiture.

TO PREPARE THE GARNISH: 1. Peel the oranges with a sharp, flexible knife, carefully removing all the white membrane. Section the oranges by sliding the knife between the membranes, removing the sections in whole pieces. Set aside. 2. Scrape off all the white pith from the orange peels to make zest. Using a very sharp knife, slice the zest as finely as possible. 3. In a small saucepan, bring about 3 cups of water and the sugar to a boil. Add the thinly sliced zest. Boil for 5 minutes and strain, discarding the liquid.

TO COOK THE LIVER AND MAKE THE SAUCE: 1. Season the liver with salt and pepper and dust with flour. 2. Place 1 tablespoon of the butter and 1 tablespoon of the oil in a large sauté pan or skillet over medium-high heat. When the butter melts and begins to color, add two slices of the liver and sauté for 2 or 3 minutes on each side, being careful not to overcook. Remove the liver. Set aside and keep warm while cooking the remaining two slices. 3. Immediately add the shallot to the hot pan, cook for one minute, then pour the stock and wine into the skillet. Boil rapidly until the liquid is reduced by half. Whisk in the cream, tomato paste, and mustard and reduce until thickened. Add the orange juice and return the sauce to a boil. Remove the pan from the heat and whisk in the remaining butter. Season with salt and pepper. Strain the sauce if desired.

TO SERVE: 1. Place one slice of liver on each of four warm serving plates. Lay orange sections on top of the liver and sprinkle the candied orange zest over the sections. 2. Place a mound of the warm onion confiture next to each piece of liver and pour a pool of the pan sauce onto each plate. Serve immediately.

4 slices calves' liver, about ½ inch thick and 7 ounces each, nicely trimmed
Salt and freshly ground pepper to taste
¼ cup all-purpose flour for dusting the liver
2 tablespoons unsalted butter
2 tablespoons olive oil

ONION CONFITURE
3 pounds large onions
3 tablespoons butter
3 tablespoons sugar
2 tablespoons fresh orange juice

GARNISH
2 navel oranges
½ cup sugar

PAN SAUCE
1 teaspoon minced shallot
½ cup chicken stock, preferably homemade (see page 170)
¼ cup white wine
¾ cup heavy cream
½ teaspoon tomato paste
1 teaspoon Dijon mustard
¼ cup fresh orange juice
1 tablespoon unsalted butter
Salt and freshly ground black pepper to taste

Roast Loin of Venison on a Tangle of Tart Greens with Black Currants and Spaetzle

The quality of fresh, farm-raised venison has greatly improved recently, and it is becoming easier to find. In general, the meat is surprisingly tender and richly flavored without any gamy taste. It's unbelievably easy to sear on top of the stove and serve, sliced over a Tangle of Tart Greens with this luscious black currant sauce. If fresh or frozen black currants are unavailable, try using blueberries. If you don't care for venison, try this dish with pork tenderloin.

Serves 6

To make the sauce: 1. In a 2-quart saucepan, melt the butter over medium heat. Add the carrot, celery, leeks, onion, bacon, and tomato paste. When the ingredients are a deep brown color, add the wine and reduce to a syrupy consistency. 2. Add the stock and reduce by one-half. 3. Add the ham and sage, simmer for 10 minutes, and strain the sauce. 4. Add the currants. Set the sauce aside and keep warm.

To prepare the venison: 1. Trim the venison. Slice the loin in half lengthwise, then into 5-inch-long portions. Season with salt and pepper. 2. In a coffee grinder or blender, coarsely grind the juniper berries and peppercorns. Sprinkle the venison with the mixture and salt liberally. 3. Heat the oil in a large, heavy-bottomed skillet over high heat and sear the venison on both sides. Reduce the heat and continue cooking for 4 to 5 minutes more, turning the meat often. The venison will taste better and be more tender if cooked rare. Remove from the pan and keep warm.

To serve: 1. Place a wreath of greens in the center of each of six warm serving plates. 2. Slice each 5-inch portion of venison into ¼-inch slices and arrange in a circle on top of the greens. Spoon a mound of sautéed Spaetzle in the center of each plate. 3. Spoon the sauce around the perimeter of the plate and serve.

2½ pounds boneless loin of venison
Salt and freshly ground pepper to taste
2 tablespoons dried juniper berries
2 tablespoons whole black peppercorns
2 tablespoons vegetable oil

Black Currant Sauce

¼ cup (½ stick) unsalted butter
1 cup chopped carrot
1 cup chopped celery
1 cup chopped leeks
1 cup chopped onion
2 strips bacon, sliced
½ tablespoon tomato paste
2 cups dry red wine
2½ cups chicken or veal stock, preferably homemade (see page 170)
2 ounces country ham, thinly sliced
1 tablespoon chopped fresh sage
½ cup fresh or frozen black currants

A Tangle of Tart Greens (see page 114)
Spaetzle (see page 119)

3 trimmed boneless veal butt tenderloins,
about 1 pound each

Salt and freshly ground pepper to taste

1 tablespoon olive oil

SAUCE

¼ cup (½ stick) unsalted butter

1 cup chopped carrot

1 cup chopped celery

1 cup chopped leeks

1 cup chopped onion

2 strips bacon, sliced

½ tablespoon tomato paste

2 cups dry red wine

2 cups veal stock, preferably homemade
(see page 170)

½ cup chicken stock, preferably
homemade (see page 170)

2 ounces Virginia country ham,
thinly sliced

1 tablespoon chopped fresh sage

GARNISH

30 pearl onions

1 cup English peas, shelled

2 tablespoons olive oil

1½ cups fresh chanterelles, stems
removed and quartered

1 tablespoon unsalted butter

1 teaspoon chopped shallot

1 teaspoon minced garlic

Salt and freshly ground pepper to taste

FETTUCCINE

1½ pounds fresh fettuccine or
1 pound dried

2 tablespoons extra-virgin olive oil

2 tablespoons Brown Butter
(see page 169)

Salt, freshly ground pepper, and
freshly grated nutmeg to taste

MEDALLIONS OF VEAL LOIN SAUTÉ WITH ENGLISH PEAS, VIRGINIA COUNTRY HAM, AND FETTUCCINE

We love the simple combination of flavors and colors in this earthy veal sauté. The great thing about using the veal butt tenderloin is that there is absolutely no waste. Any good-quality dried or fresh fettuccine may be used, and sugar snap peas make an excellent substitute when fresh peas are not in season. Frozen peas will also work. Any fresh mushrooms can be substituted for the chanterelles. If you can't locate the inimitable Virginia country ham, use thinly sliced boiled ham.

SERVES 6

TO MAKE THE SAUCE: **1.** In a 2-quart saucepan, melt the butter over medium heat. Add the carrot, celery, leeks, onion, bacon, and tomato paste. **2.** When the ingredients are a deep brown color, add the wine and reduce almost to a syrup. **3.** Add the veal and chicken stocks. Reduce again by one-half. **4.** Add the ham and sage and simmer for 10 minutes. **5.** Strain the sauce. Set aside and keep warm.

TO MAKE THE GARNISH: **1.** In a large pot, bring 4 quarts of water to a boil. Add the onions and boil for 2 minutes. Drain, peel the onions, and reserve. **2.** In a medium-size saucepan, bring 2 cups of water to a boil. Add the peas and boil for 3 to 4 minutes, or until just tender. Drain and plunge into ice water to set their color and stop the cooking. Drain again. **3.** Place a 12-inch sauté pan over high heat and add the oil. When the oil is smoking hot, add the chanterelles and sauté until crisp and lightly browned, about 2 minutes. **4.** Add the onions, butter, shallot, garlic, and salt and pepper. Add the peas and sauté over low heat until the peas are just warmed through.

TO COOK THE FETTUCCINE: **1.** Meanwhile, in a large pot, bring 6 quarts of salted water to a boil. Add the fettuccine and cook for about 2 minutes for fresh or 4 minutes for dried. **2.** Drain the pasta and place in a large bowl. Add the oil and Brown Butter. Season with salt, pepper, and nutmeg.

TO COOK THE VEAL: **1.** Slice the tenderloins into 1-inch rounds and season with salt and pepper. **2.** Cover the bottom of a 12-inch sauté pan with the oil. Heat until almost smoking, then sear the veal on both sides until golden brown. **3.** Reduce the heat and continue cooking until the meat is cooked through but still a bit pink in the center.

TO SERVE: Swirl the dressed fettuccine across each of six hot plates or arrange on a serving platter in a swath about 2 inches wide. Arrange the veal on the pasta and place the garnish on top. Ladle the sauce around the plate, spooning a little on top of the noodles.

3 pairs veal sweetbreads
(about 3 pounds)
2 quarts chicken stock (see page 170)
1 teaspoon salt, plus more to
season sweetbreads
Freshly ground pepper
¼ cup flour
½ pound (2 sticks) unsalted butter
¾ teaspoon fresh lemon juice
36 snow peas, washed and stringed
Pinch of sugar
12 large fresh mushrooms, sliced

MUSTARD SAUCE
1 cup Chablis or other dry white wine
1 shallot, finely minced
1 teaspoon Dijon mustard
1 teaspoon whole-grain mustard
1 teaspoon green herb mustard
1 cup heavy cream
½ teaspoon minced garlic
Salt and freshly ground pepper

SCALLOPINI OF VEAL SWEETBREADS SAUTÉ WITH THREE-MUSTARD SAUCE

This method of cooking sweetbreads gives the meat a dual texture: a crispy exterior and a meltingly tender interior, almost like fried mozzarella. Surprisingly, even people who are not sweetbread fans enjoy this preparation immensely, since what they usually find objectionable about sweetbreads is the squishy texture. For added interest, we combine them with scallopini of veal. The sharp mustard sauce and crunchy snow peas complement the sweetbreads' delicate flavor and texture.

Most of the preparation can be done well in advance. Weighting the poached sweetbreads firms them up, making it easier to slice them. If necessary, the sweetbread slices may be placed between two sheets of waxed paper and tapped gently with the side of a cleaver to make them thinner. Be careful not to overcook them, as they will become dry.

In the old days, this mustard sauce was enriched with sauce charon, a tarragon-flavored hollandaise we always had handy. These days we're more likely to serve the sweetbread scallopinis as a warm salad without a sauce, resting on a bed of baby lettuces dressed with sherry vinegar.

SERVES 6

PREPARING THE SWEETBREADS:
1. Rinse the sweetbreads and cover them with cold water. Place in the refrigerator overnight, covered with plastic wrap. The next day, pull off the white membrane encasing the sweetbreads. **2.** Place the chicken stock in a 2-quart saucepan and bring to a boil. Add the sweetbreads, turn the heat down to a simmer, and poach about 10 minutes over medium heat, or until the lobes spring back to the touch. **3.** Remove the sweetbreads with a slotted spoon and plunge them into a bowl of ice water to stop the cooking. Rinse well, place in a colander over a bowl, and set a plate weighted with two or three soup cans on top of the sweetbreads. Refrigerate for several hours or overnight. **4.** Slice the sweetbreads into thin slices (about ¼ inch thick) and sprinkle them lightly with salt and pepper. Dust with flour and set aside. **5.** In a sauté pan or 12-inch skillet, melt 3 tablespoons of the butter over high heat. Add the sweetbreads and sauté on both sides until golden brown. Repeat until all slices are fried, adding more butter as necessary. Remove to a warm platter, sprinkle lightly with lemon juice, and keep warm in a low oven. **6.** Meanwhile, blanch the snow peas in 2 quarts boiling salted

water for one minute. Drain and plunge into a bowl of ice water. Melt 2 tablespoons of the butter in another sauté pan. When the foam starts to subside, add the snow peas and season with the sugar, ½ teaspoon salt, and a pinch of pepper. Sauté until just warmed through and coated with butter. Remove with a slotted spoon and set aside. **7.** Wipe the mushrooms with a damp cloth and slice them thin. Melt 3 tablespoons of the butter in the same sauté pan over high heat. Add the mushrooms and season with ½ teaspoon salt and a pinch of pepper. Sauté about 3 minutes, or until they are cooked but still firm. Remove and set aside.

TO MAKE THE SAUCE: In a small saucepan, cook the wine and shallot over high heat until the liquid is reduced to 2 tablespoons. Stir in the mustards and cream, and bring the mixture to a boil, reducing for 5 minutes over medium heat. Add the garlic and return the sauce to a boil, stirring until thickened. Adjust seasonings. Set aside.

TO SERVE: **1.** On each of six serving plates, alternate the slices of sweetbreads with the snow peas in an overlapping circle and sprinkle the sautéed mushrooms on top. **2.** Ladle the mustard sauce around the sweetbreads and pass additional sauce at the table.

3 trimmed boneless veal butt tenderloins,
about 1 pound each

Salt and freshly ground pepper to taste

1 tablespoon olive oil

¼ cup apple cider, preferably
unpasteurized

2 tablespoons calvados

CALVADOS CREAM

1 tablespoon butter

1 cup chopped white mushrooms

1 teaspoon minced garlic

1 tablespoon chopped shallot

2 tablespoons coarsely chopped fresh
Italian parsley

2 tablespoons stemmed and coarsely
chopped fresh rosemary

¾ cup veal stock, preferably homemade
(see page 170)

1½ cups apple cider, preferably
unpasteurized

1 quart heavy cream

Salt and white pepper to taste

2 tablespoons calvados

GARNISHES

2 tablespoons butter

2 Granny Smith or Golden Delicious
apples, peeled, cored, and carved into
18 "turned" sections

2 tablespoons sugar

2 tablespoons calvados

6 pitted prunes

Apple cider, preferably unpasteurized

FETTUCCINE

1 pound fresh fettuccine or ¾ pound dried

1 tablespoon extra-virgin olive oil

1 tablespoon Brown Butter
(see page 169)

Pinch of freshly grated nutmeg

Salt and freshly ground pepper to taste

½ cup coarsely chopped walnuts, toasted

MEDALLIONS OF VEAL SHENANDOAH WITH CALVADOS CREAM AND FETTUCCINE WITH WALNUTS

Every fall during apple season, Veal Shenandoah (named in honor of the regional mountains) returns to our menu in a slightly different and more evolved guise. It used to be a simple veal scallopini with a pan sauce made of reduced apple cider and a cinnamon stick. Next we added a splash of cream, and then the scallopini became medallions of veal tenderloin.

However you serve it, the combination of veal and apples is always wonderful. We serve it with homemade fettuccine or Spaetzle (see page 119). Garnishes are carved apples and prunes steeped in cider. Veal scallopini may be used instead of the veal butt tenderloins.

SERVES 6

TO MAKE THE CALVADOS CREAM: **1.** In a 4-quart heavy-bottomed saucepan, melt the butter over medium heat. Add mushrooms, garlic, shallot, parsley, and rosemary and sweat for about 5 minutes. **2.** Add the stock and reduce over medium-high heat for about 8 minutes, or until slightly thickened. Add the cider and reduce again for 10 to 12 minutes. **3.** Add the cream, bring to a rapid boil, and then reduce the heat to a simmer. Cook for 6 to 8 minutes. **4.** Remove from the heat and pass through a fine strainer, pressing hard to extract the juices from the solids. Season with salt and white pepper. Add the calvados. Keep warm until ready to serve.

TO MAKE THE GARNISHES: **1.** In a medium-size sauté pan, heat the butter over medium heat until it just begins to color. Add the apples and sprinkle with the sugar. Sauté until the apples begin to caramelize and turn golden brown. **2.** Averting your face, add the calvados. The apples will ignite briefly. When the flames subside, remove the apples from the pan and keep warm. **3.** Place the prunes in a small bowl and add apple cider to cover. Let steep for ½ hour or more, then cut into slices.

TO COOK THE FETTUCCINE: **1.** In a large pot, bring 6 quarts of salted water to a boil. Add the fettuccine and cook for about 2 minutes for fresh or 4 minutes for dried. **2.** Drain the pasta and place in a large bowl. Add the oil, Brown Butter, and nutmeg. Season with salt and pepper. Toss in the walnuts.

TO COOK THE VEAL: **1.** Slice the veal into 1-inch rounds and season with salt and pepper. **2.** Cover the bottom of a 12-inch sauté pan with the oil. Heat until almost smoking, then sear the veal on both sides until golden brown. **3.** In a small bowl, combine the cider and calvados and add to the hot pan. Cook until the meat absorbs the liquid and is cooked through but still a bit pink in the center.

TO SERVE: Place a mound of the dressed fettuccine on each of six hot plates or on a serving platter. Surround the noodles with the veal medallions interspersed with the apple and prune garnishes. Ladle the calvados cream around the plate.

Portobello Mushrooms Pretending to Be a Filet Mignon

This vegetarian main course will satisfy an avid carnivore. Grilled portobello mushroom caps are layered with Roasted Tomato and Shallot Fondue, placed on a nest of charred onions and vegetable ribbons, mounded with Wild Rice Pecan Pilaf, and sauced with Tomato Coulis. Serve with steak knives!

SERVES 4

TO CHAR THE ONIONS AND COOK THE VEGETABLE RIBBONS:
1. Heat a cast-iron skillet over high heat until very hot.   2. Moisten the onion slices with the oil and lay them in the hot skillet one layer deep. Cook until lightly charred, turn over with tongs, and char the other side. Remove from the pan and keep warm. Repeat until all the onions are cooked.   3. Meanwhile, bring about 2 quarts of lightly salted water to a rapid boil and drop in the carrot ribbons. Cook for 2 to 3 minutes, or until the carrots are tender but still al dente. Lift the carrots out of the water with a slotted spoon and place in a bowl. Using the same pot of boiling water, repeat this process with the zucchini ribbons. (Note: The zucchini will cook much faster than the carrots.)   4. Add the cooked zucchini to the carrots. Add the Brown Butter and season with salt and pepper.

TO GRILL THE MUSHROOMS: 1. Preheat the grill or broiler.   2. Using a 4-inch round cookie cutter, stamp out or trim each mushroom cap into a perfect circle. (Save the trimmings for another use.)   3. Place the trimmed mushroom caps in a shallow baking pan. Pour the ¼ cup oil over them and sprinkle with the garlic. Lightly season with salt and pepper and toss the mushrooms in the oil to coat evenly.   4. Grill or broil the mushrooms for about 3½ minutes per side. Remove from the grill or broiler and keep warm.

TO SERVE: 1. Heat the Tomato Coulis and Roasted Tomato and Shallot Fondue.   2. Lay three or four charred onion rings in the center of each of four warm serving plates. Arrange two slices of cooked carrot and two slices of cooked zucchini over the onion rings in a nestlike pattern. Place a mound of Wild Rice Pecan Pilaf in the center of the vegetables.   3. Turn four of the grilled mushroom caps upside down and spread about 2 tablespoons of Roasted Tomato and Shallot Fondue on the bottom of each cap. Place another cap right side up on top, forming a "sandwich." Set the filled mushroom caps on top of the wild rice.   4. Spoon the Tomato Coulis around the plate and serve.

TOMATO COULIS

MAKES APPROXIMATELY 1¼ CUPS

Place all ingredients in a medium-size saucepan and bring to a boil. Simmer uncovered for 20 minutes. Puree and strain.

---

8 portobello mushroom caps, each about 4½ inches in diameter

¼ cup olive oil

½ teaspoon minced garlic

Salt and freshly ground pepper to taste

CHARRED ONIONS AND VEGETABLE RIBBONS

1 large white onion, sliced ¼ inch thick

4 tablespoons olive oil

2 large carrots, peeled and sliced ⅛ inch thick lengthwise into ribbons

2 medium zucchini, sliced ⅛ inch thick lengthwise into ribbons

2 tablespoons Brown Butter (see page 169)

Salt and freshly ground pepper to taste

Tomato Coulis (recipe follows)

Roasted Tomato and Shallot Fondue (see page 115)

Wild Rice Pecan Pilaf (see page 115)

1 carrot, peeled and coarsely chopped

½ stalk celery, coarsely chopped

¼ onion, coarsely chopped

½ leek, coarsely chopped

1 cup tomato juice

½ cup diced tomato

1 tablespoon tomato paste

1 bay leaf

6 fresh basil leaves

RACK OF BABY LAMB ON NEW POTATOES WITH BARLEY AND WILD MUSHROOMS

Barley adds a unique touch to the stock reduction sauce that accompanies this full-flavored but relatively light and healthful lamb preparation. The smallest racks available are marinated in olive oil, mustard, and herbs, then roasted, sliced, and placed on new potatoes, wild mushrooms, and Oven-Roasted Plum Tomatoes. The lamb is sauced with a rich broth containing barley and roast garlic and garnished with a mixture of sautéed wild mushrooms.

SERVES 4

1. Trim the lamb of fat and split each rack in two, leaving the bones in place. **2.** In a small bowl, whisk together the oil, mustard, and pepper. Add the garlic and thyme. **3.** Rub the lamb with the marinade. Cover and refrigerate overnight.

TO MAKE THE SAUCE: 1. In a 4-quart saucepan, heat the oil over medium-high heat. Add the onion, chopped carrot, and celery. Cook until the vegetables begin to brown. Add the wine, tomato paste, and lamb and chicken stocks. Reduce the heat and simmer for 1½ hours, occasionally skimming the foam off the top. **2.** Strain the sauce and set aside. **3.** Put the barley in a strainer and rinse well under cold running water. Place in a small saucepan and add enough water to cover the barley by a depth of 3 inches. Bring to a simmer and cook for 45 minutes, or until the barley is tender. Drain. **4.** Add the cooked barley and roasted garlic to the lamb sauce. **5.** In a small saucepan, bring about 2 cups of lightly salted water to a boil. Cook the diced carrot for about 3 minutes, or until just tender. Drain and add to the sauce.

TO PREPARE THE POTATOES AND MUSHROOMS: 1. Place 4 washed and unpeeled new potatoes in a medium-size saucepan and cover with cold salted water. Bring to a boil and cook for about 10 minutes. Drain, cool, and slice the potatoes ¼ inch thick. **2.** In a sauté pan, sauté the potato slices in oil until they are golden brown. Season with salt and pepper. **3.** Trim any coarse or dirty stems off the mushrooms. Film a 10-inch skillet with oil and place over high heat. Add the mushrooms and butter. Sauté until the mushrooms are crisp. Add the shallot and season with salt and pepper. Sauté for 30 seconds more, remove the mushrooms from pan, and keep warm.

TO COOK THE LAMB: 1. Preheat the oven to 400 degrees. **2.** Roast the lamb racks for about 10 minutes (for medium-rare). Remove from the oven and let rest for 5 minutes.

TO SERVE: 1. Place the potatoes and mushrooms in a mound in the center of each of four warm serving plates. Lay one whole roasted tomato on top. **2.** Run a sharp knife between the bones of the lamb rack and slice off four chops. Remove the rest of the meat from the bone and slice into ½-inch-thick medallions. Place the medallions around the potatoes and mushrooms and lay a single whole chop, bone up, against the roasted tomato. **3.** Spoon the hot barley sauce around the plate and serve immediately.

---

2 racks of lamb, about 1 pound each

MARINADE

¼ cup olive oil

¼ cup Dijon mustard

Freshly ground pepper to taste

2 cloves garlic, crushed

2 sprigs fresh thyme

SAUCE

¼ cup olive oil

1 small onion, coarsely chopped

1 carrot, peeled and coarsely chopped

2 stalks celery, coarsely chopped

¼ cup red wine

1 tablespoon tomato paste

1 cup lamb stock

3 cups chicken stock, preferably homemade (see page 170)

½ cup uncooked barley

1 tablespoon roasted garlic (see instructions on page 116)

¼ cup finely diced carrot

POTATOES AND MUSHROOMS

4 small red new potatoes

¼ cup olive oil (approximately)

Salt and freshly ground pepper to taste

1½ cups wild mushrooms, such as chanterelles, morels, or oyster mushrooms

1 tablespoon butter

1 teaspoon finely minced shallot

Oven-Roasted Plum Tomatoes (see page 108)

RABBIT BRAISED IN APPLE CIDER

Our unique regional products are combined and enhanced using classical French cooking techniques in this earthy but elegant braised rabbit dish. The rabbit meat is removed from the bone, the legs are braised for an hour or so in chicken stock and fresh apple cider, and the rabbit loins are seared and cooked just before serving. This method allows the leg to emerge full-flavored and wonderfully tender and keeps the little loins from drying out. Removing the meat from the carcass is not difficult, but your butcher or rabbit merchant may be willing to do this for you. Note that the rabbit stock needs to be made a day in advance. If you don't want to bother, simply omit that procedure and substitute chicken stock.

We are lucky enough to have rabbits raised for us organically by a local farmer, so we can specify the age and size we want. (We generally use rabbits that are about 8 weeks old and weigh about 3 pounds.) If you don't have a source for rabbits, try this recipe using chicken instead.

SERVES 6

TO MAKE THE STOCK: **1.** The day before you wish to serve the dish, preheat the oven to 350 degrees. **2.** Remove the hind legs and loins from the rabbits. Wrap them in plastic wrap, keeping the loins separate from the legs, and refrigerate. **3.** Roughly chop the rabbit carcasses. Film a large roasting pan with oil and add the carcasses. Roast for about 30 minutes, or until deep brown in color. **4.** Meanwhile, place a large, heavy-bottomed stockpot over medium heat. Add the remaining oil, onion, and carrot. Cook, stirring often, until the vegetables are browned. Add the tomato paste, red wine, celery, bay leaves, parsley, peppercorns, thyme, and tomato. **5.** Add the browned rabbit bones to the stockpot, scraping the roasting pan with a rubber spatula to remove any pieces sticking to the bottom. Pour about 1 cup of hot water into the roasting pan, set it over high heat, and boil for 1 minute to release any of the flavorful bits remaining. Add the water to the stockpot. **6.** Add enough cold water to the stockpot to cover the bones by 1 inch. Bring the stock to a gentle boil, skimming off any foam rising to the surface. Lower the heat and simmer for 4 hours. **7.** Strain the stock and refrigerate overnight.

TO BRAISE THE LEGS: **1.** Preheat the oven to 350 degrees. **2.** Remove the rabbit legs from the refrigerator and season generously with salt and pepper. **3.** In a very large skillet or sauté pan set over medium-high heat, brown the bacon pieces. Remove the bacon with a slotted spoon and reserve. **4.** Add the oil to the bacon fat in the pan and brown the rabbit legs on both sides until they are a deep golden brown. Remove the legs with tongs and keep warm. **5.** Add the onion, carrot, and celery to the pan and brown the vegetables. **6.** Add the cider, bay leaves, parsley, peppercorns, and tomato. Place the browned rabbit legs on top of the vegetables and cover with the chicken stock. Cover the pan with aluminum foil and bake for 1½ hours. **7.** Meanwhile, remove the rabbit stock from the refrigerator and skim off all the fat. **8.** Remove the pan from the oven. Carefully

---

3 rabbits, about 3 pounds each

RABBIT STOCK
¼ cup olive oil (approximately)
1 cup coarsely chopped onion
1 cup coarsely chopped carrot
1 tablespoon tomato paste
½ cup dry red wine
1 cup coarsely chopped celery
2 bay leaves
6 sprigs fresh parsley
2 tablespoons whole black peppercorns
2 sprigs fresh thyme
1 tomato, peeled, seeded, and chopped

FOR BRAISING THE RABBITS
Salt and freshly ground pepper
2 strips thick bacon, cut into 12 pieces
¼ cup olive oil
½ cup coarsely chopped onion
½ cup coarsely chopped carrot
½ cup coarsely chopped celery
¾ cup apple cider
2 bay leaves
4 sprigs fresh parsley
1 tablespoon whole black peppercorns
½ cup peeled, seeded, and diced tomato
1 quart chicken stock, preferably homemade (see page 170), heated to a simmer

FOR COOKING THE LOINS
Salt and freshly ground pepper to taste
3 tablespoons olive oil
½ cup stemmed and diced shiitake mushrooms
½ cup stemmed and sliced oyster mushrooms
¼ cup peeled, seeded, and diced tomato
⅓ cup dried black currants
18 pearl onions, blanched until tender and peeled
¼ cup apple cider, preferably unpasteurized
½ cup apple brandy
2 tablespoons unsalted butter

Garlic Mashed Potatoes (see page 119)

lift out the legs and keep warm. Strain the braising liquid and combine it with the rabbit stock in a large saucepan over high heat. Boil until reduced by one-half. Set aside.

TO COOK THE LOINS: 1. Remove the rabbit loins from the refrigerator and season with salt and pepper. Add the oil to a large skillet and sauté the loins over high heat until lightly browned.   2. Add the shiitake and oyster mushrooms, tomato, currants, pearl onions, and reserved bacon. Remove from the heat and add the cider and brandy, being careful not to let it ignite. Add just enough of the reduced braising liquid to cover the loins. Simmer until the loins are just firm to the touch, about 3 minutes. Remove the loins from the pan and keep warm.   3. Reduce the liquid in the pan until it thickens slightly. Swirl in the butter and adjust the seasoning.

TO SERVE: 1. Slice the loins on an angle into four or five pieces.   2. In the center of each of six warm serving plates, place an oval of Garlic Mashed Potatoes. Arrange a leg and one sliced loin around the potatoes. Spoon the reduced pan sauce over and around the rabbits, dividing the bacon, pearl onions, and currants evenly among the plates.

LOIN OF LAMB IN A FRAGRANT BROTH WITH GREMOLATA

Gremolata is simply an old Italian combination of minced herbs, lemon peel, and garlic and is the traditional garnish for osso buco (braised veal shanks). The intensive flavor of this simple, healthful combination is startling and a great accent for lamb. In this dish, the loin of lamb is removed from the bone, marinated, seared, sliced, and served in a clear lamb broth sprinkled with gremolata. It's not absolutely necessary to clarify the broth, but it adds to the visual appeal of the dish. The vegetables take on a jewel-like appearance floating in the clear amber liquid.

SERVES 4

1. Place the lamb loins in a nonreactive pan. **2.** In a small bowl, combine the vegetable oil, olive oil, rosemary, pepper, bay leaves, and garlic. Pour over the lamb, cover, and refrigerate overnight.

TO MAKE THE BROTH: 1. Preheat the oven to 400 degrees. Film a roasting pan with oil and add the lamb bones. Roast until browned, about 45 minutes. **2.** Heat the remaining oil in a 6-quart heavy-bottomed saucepan over medium-high heat. Add the onion, carrot, and celery and cook for about 8 minutes, or until the vegetables turn brown. **3.** Add the roasted bones and water to the pan. Simmer for about 2 hours, occasionally skimming foam off the top, until reduced to about 8 cups. Strain, cool, and refrigerate overnight.

TO CLARIFY THE BROTH: 1. Remove the broth from refrigerator and skim the fat from the surface. Transfer to a 6-quart heavy-bottomed saucepan. Add the lamb, tomato, carrot, celery, onion, parsley, and bay leaves. Bring to a simmer. **2.** In a medium-size bowl, whisk the egg whites. Whisk in 1 cup of the broth. Return this mixture to the pot and bring to a simmer, whisking gently. Stop whisking and simmer very gently for 30 minutes. **3.** Set a strainer lined with cheesecloth over a large saucepan and gently ladle the broth into the strainer. Simmer the strained broth for about 30 minutes, or until reduced to 4 cups. Keep hot.

TO MAKE THE GREMOLATA: In a small bowl, combine the parsley, lemon zest, garlic, and rosemary. Set aside.

TO MAKE THE VEGETABLE GARNISH: 1. Cook the potato in a small pan of boiling water until just tender. Drain and set aside. **2.** Cook the carrot in a small pan of boiling water for 2 minutes. Add the zucchini and cook for about 2 minutes more. Drain and combine with the potato. Keep warm.

2 racks of lamb, about 1¼ pounds each (Ask your butcher to remove the loins from the bone. Keep the bones to make stock.)

MARINADE
½ cup vegetable oil
½ cup olive oil
1 teaspoon dried rosemary, crumbled
1 teaspoon freshly ground pepper
2 bay leaves, crumbled
3 cloves garlic, chopped

BROTH
¼ cup vegetable oil (approximately)
3 pounds lamb bones
1 onion, chopped
1 carrot, chopped
1 stalk celery, chopped
3½ quarts water

CLARIFYING THE BROTH
¼ pound lean ground lamb
1 cup peeled, seeded, and chopped tomato
¼ cup chopped carrot
¼ cup chopped celery
¼ cup chopped onion
½ bunch fresh parsley
3 bay leaves
4 egg whites

GREMOLATA
¼ cup minced fresh parsley
2 teaspoons grated lemon zest
4 cloves garlic, minced
2 teaspoons minced fresh rosemary

VEGETABLE GARNISHES
¼ cup peeled and diced potato
¼ cup peeled and diced carrot
¼ cup diced zucchini
¼ cup peeled, seeded, and diced tomato

TO COOK THE LAMB: Remove the lamb from the marinade. Heat a large, heavy skillet over medium-high heat. Add the lamb loins and cook for about 8 minutes (for medium-rare), turning frequently. Transfer the lamb to a cutting board and slice into ¼-inch medallions.

TO SERVE: **1.** Place half of a sliced lamb loin in a circle in the center of each of four warm shallow bowls. **2.** Ladle the hot broth around the lamb and divide the diced vegetables evenly among the bowls, sprinkling in the diced tomato last. **3.** In the center of each bowl, place a small mound of gremolata. Serve immediately.

BONELESS RACK OF LAMB IN A PECAN CRUST WITH BARBECUE SAUCE AND SHOESTRING SWEET POTATOES

Through the years, this has been one of our most popular versions of rack of lamb. The racks are brushed with barbecue sauce, grilled, boned, rolled in more sauce, and then rolled in crushed pecans. The meat is then sliced into medallions and served with crispy Shoestring Sweet Potatoes and Sautéed Fresh Green Beans. The sauce is simply a red wine reduction enhanced by a Southern barbecue sauce.

SERVES 6

3 racks of lamb, about 1½ pounds each with 8 rib bones
Salt and freshly ground pepper to taste
½ cup coarsely chopped pecans, toasted

BARBECUE SAUCE
1 cup ketchup
1 medium-size onion, quartered
½ cup white wine vinegar
¼ cup Worcestershire sauce
2 teaspoons dry mustard
1 teaspoon Tabasco
½ cup firmly packed brown sugar

RED WINE SAUCE
1 tablespoon vegetable oil
⅓ cup chopped white mushrooms
1 carrot, peeled and coarsely chopped
1 stalk celery, coarsely chopped
½ onion, coarsely chopped
1 shallot, coarsely chopped
¼ cup all-purpose flour
1 clove garlic, minced
2 tablespoons chopped fresh parsley
2 teaspoons chopped fresh rosemary
2 teaspoons chopped fresh tarragon
2 bay leaves
2 quarts chicken stock, preferably homemade (see page 170) or water
2 cups red wine (such as cabernet sauvignon)
2 tablespoons tomato paste
1 tomato, peeled, seeded, and chopped
Salt and freshly ground pepper to taste

Shoestring Sweet Potatoes (recipe follows)
Sautéed Fresh Green Beans (see page 108)

TO MAKE THE BARBECUE SAUCE: In the bowl of a food processor fitted with a steel blade, puree the ketchup, onion, vinegar, Worcestershire sauce, mustard, Tabasco, and brown sugar. Set aside. (This sauce may be made several days in advance and kept refrigerated.)

TO MAKE THE RED WINE SAUCE: **1.** In a 6-quart heavy-bottomed stockpot, heat the oil over medium-high heat. Add the mushrooms, carrot, celery, onion, and shallot and cook until the vegetables are a deep golden brown. **2.** Add the flour and cook for 5 to 6 minutes, stirring to prevent sticking. **3.** Add the garlic, parsley, rosemary, tarragon, bay leaves, stock or water, red wine, tomato paste, tomato, and salt and pepper. Simmer for 1½ hours, stirring occasionally, until reduced by one-half. Adjust the seasonings and strain. **4.** For each cup of strained wine sauce, add 2 tablespoons of barbecue sauce. (This sauce may be made several days in advance and kept refrigerated.)

TO COOK THE LAMB: **1.** Preheat the oven to 400 degrees. **2.** Season the lamb with salt and pepper and brush each side with the basic barbecue sauce. **3.** Grill or broil the lamb enough to crisp and lightly char the exterior on all sides. **4.** Place the lamb in a roasting pan and finish baking for about 14 to 15 minutes (for medium-rare). **5.** Remove the lamb, place on a cutting board, and let rest for 5 minutes. Lay the blade of a sharp knife against the bone and slip the meat off in one piece. **6.** Roll the boneless loins first in the basic barbecue sauce, then in the pecans. Slice each loin into 6 medallions.

TO SERVE: **1.** Reheat the barbecue-flavored red wine sauce. . **2.** Place three medallions on each of six hot serving plates. Dribble the wine sauce over the plate and place a mound of Shoestring Sweet Potatoes in the middle of each plate. Garnish with Sautéed Fresh Green Beans.

SHOESTRING SWEET POTATOES

It is essential to use a mandolin to cut the potatoes finely enough that they resemble crispy string after cooking. The shoestrings will appear somewhat limp when first removed from the oil, but they will become crisp as they dry.

SERVES 6

1. Heat the oil to 350 degrees in a deep pot. **2.** Sprinkle the potatoes into the oil and stir. Cook for 20 to 30 seconds. **3.** Using a slotted spoon, remove the potatoes from the oil and drain on paper towels. Sprinkle with salt.

NOTE: If you are not using the potatoes immediately, store them in an airtight container in a cool, dry place.

*1 large sweet potato, peeled and
very finely julienned*
2 quarts peanut or vegetable oil
Salt to taste

RAINBOW TROUT IN A POTATO CRUST

Local rainbow trout is always on our breakfast menu at The Inn, and this is one of our favorite adaptations. The trout is filleted and coated with thin slices of new potato. When fried, the crispy potato "crust" looks like fish scales. For breakfast, we serve half a trout. As a dinner main course, 2 fillets per person is ideal.

SERVES 2 TO 4

1. Remove the heads from the trout and fillet the fish, using tweezers or fish pliers to remove all the pin bones. Remove the skin from the fillets. Lay the fillets on individual squares of waxed paper and sprinkle with salt and white pepper. **2.** Slice the unpeeled potatoes about 1/16 inch thick and lay them in an overlapping "fish scale" pattern on the surface of the fillets. **3.** Film a 10-inch skillet or sauté pan with oil over medium-high heat. Gently lift each fillet by sliding one hand underneath the waxed paper and carefully flipping the fillet over into the pan (potato side down), being careful not to splash the hot oil. Add more oil to the pan so that the potato "scales" are immersed. Cook for 3 minutes, or until the edges of the potatoes begin to turn golden brown. Using a perforated spatula, gently turn the fillets over and cook for 1 minute more.

TO SERVE: Remove the fillets from the pan and place on warm serving plates. Sprinkle with the parsley and garnish with the lemon wedges. Serve immediately.

*2 whole rainbow trout,
about 18 ounces each*
Salt and white pepper to taste
Vegetable oil
8 small red new potatoes
2 tablespoons finely chopped fresh parsley
Lemon wedges

STEAMED LOBSTER WITH GRAPEFRUIT BUTTER SAUCE

This is a refreshingly different treatment for lobster. The grapefruit juice in the sauce offsets the richness of the lobster, and the butter keeps the citrus from being too sharp. Garnishes of fresh grapefruit sections and blanched spinach add a healthful note. The colors and flavors in this dish are electrifying.

SERVES 4

TO COOK THE LOBSTERS: **1.** Holding the lobsters with a kitchen towel, carefully pull off the claws. **2.** In a large kettle or steamer, bring 2 inches of salted water to a rolling boil. Add the lobster bodies, cover, and cook for 1 minute. Add the claws, cover, and cook for 8 minutes more. **3.** Remove the lobsters and their claws from the steamer and plunge into ice water for 3 minutes to stop the cooking. **4.** Remove the lobsters from the ice water. Pull out the tail and claw meat in whole pieces, using a mallet to crack the claws. Refrigerate the meat.

TO COOK THE ORZO: **1.** In a large saucepan, bring 3 quarts of salted water to a rolling boil and add the orzo. Cook for 5 minutes, or until al dente. **2.** Drain the orzo and transfer to a medium-size bowl. Add the Brown Butter, oil, nutmeg, and salt and white pepper. Toss gently to coat the pasta evenly. Set aside and keep warm.

TO MAKE THE SPINACH SAUTÉ: In a large skillet, melt the butter over medium heat. When the butter begins to foam, add the spinach and quickly toss with tongs to coat evenly. Add the nutmeg and season with salt and pepper. Remove to a warm dish.

TO MAKE THE SAUCE: **1.** In a 2-quart heavy-bottomed saucepan, combine the grapefruit juice, cream, and stock. Cook over medium-high heat until it has a syrupy consistency. **2.** Whisk in the cold butter, 1 tablespoon at a time, until all the butter is incorporated. Season with salt and white pepper. Set aside and keep warm.

TO SERVE: **1.** In a 4-quart saucepan, combine 1 quart of water with the orange juice and butter. Bring to a simmer. **2.** Drop the lobster meat into the pan and warm for 2 minutes. **3.** Meanwhile, place a mound of the dressed orzo in the center of each of four hot serving plates. **4.** Remove the lobster meat from the pan with a slotted spoon and distribute among the plates on top of the orzo. Garnish with grapefruit sections and spinach sauté and surround with Grapefruit Butter Sauce.

NOTE: The lobsters may be steamed and removed from their shells well in advance and kept refrigerated until ready to serve. The sauce may be made an hour or so ahead of time and kept warm in the top of a double boiler off the heat. Steamed white rice may be substituted for the orzo.

4 lobsters, about 1½ pounds each

ORZO
1 cup uncooked orzo
2 tablespoons Brown Butter (see page 169)
2 tablespoons extra-virgin olive oil
Pinch of freshly grated nutmeg
Salt and white pepper to taste

SPINACH SAUTÉ
3 tablespoons butter
2 cups tightly packed spinach leaves, stems removed
Pinch of freshly grated nutmeg
Salt and freshly ground pepper to taste

GRAPEFRUIT BUTTER SAUCE
Juice of 4 pink grapefruits
1 cup heavy cream
¾ cup chicken stock, preferably homemade (see page 170)
1 cup (2 sticks) cold unsalted butter, cut into tablespoon-size pieces
Salt and white pepper to taste

FLAVORED LIQUID TO REWARM THE LOBSTERS
1 quart water
1 cup orange juice
3 tablespoons butter

GRAPEFRUIT GARNISH
2 grapefruits, peeled, carefully sectioned, and pith removed

93

4 center-cut tuna steaks, about
6 ounces each, trimmed into the
shape of filet mignon

1 large white onion, sliced ¼ inch thick

¼ cup olive oil (approximately)

2 large carrots, peeled and sliced very
thin lengthwise into ribbons

2 medium-size zucchini, sliced very
thin lengthwise into ribbons

2 tablespoons Brown Butter
(see page 169)

Salt and freshly ground pepper to taste

4 ounces foie gras

Burgundy Butter Sauce (recipe follows)

"FILET MIGNON" OF RARE TUNA CAPPED WITH SEARED FOIE GRAS ON CHARRED ONIONS AND A BURGUNDY BUTTER SAUCE

Tuna lends itself well to some of the same methods used for cooking beef. This preparation could confuse a blindfolded cowboy into thinking he was biting into a succulent steak. In this dish, a center-cut portion of tuna is trimmed to resemble a filet mignon, grilled rare, topped with a slab of seared foie gras (fattened duck liver), and sauced with an explosively full-flavored red wine sauce. It's served resting on charred onions and ribbons of zucchini and carrot. Naturally, the same concept works beautifully with a fillet of beef. If foie gras is unavailable, just omit it. The dish will still be sensational without it.

SERVES 4

1. Heat a 10-inch cast-iron skillet over high heat until very hot. **2.** Moisten the onion slices with oil and lay in the hot skillet one layer deep. Cook until lightly charred, turn over with tongs, and char the other side. Remove from the pan and keep warm. Repeat until all the onions are cooked. **3.** Meanwhile, bring about 2 quarts of lightly salted water to a rapid boil and drop in the carrot ribbons. Cook for 2 to 3 minutes, or until the carrots are tender but still al dente. Lift the carrots out of the water with a slotted spoon and place in a bowl. Using the same pot of boiling water, repeat this process with the zucchini ribbons. (Note: The zucchini will cook much faster than the carrots.) **4.** Add the cooked zucchini to the carrots. Add the Brown Butter and season with salt and pepper. **5.** Using a very sharp knife dipped in warm water, cut the foie gras into ½-inch-thick slices. Sprinkle with salt and pepper and keep chilled. **6.** Moisten the tuna steaks with oil and season with salt and pepper. Place into the same hot skillet used to char the onions. Sear for about 2 minutes on each side. Remove and keep warm. **7.** In a smoking-hot 7-inch sauté pan, sear the liver slices on both sides for about 30 seconds, or just until a crisp outer crust forms. Remove and keep warm.

TO SERVE: 1. Quickly lay three or four charred onion rings in the center of each of four warm serving plates. Arrange two carrot ribbons and two zucchini ribbons over the onions in a nestlike pattern. Place a tuna steak on top, then finish with a slice of foie gras and a few charred onions. **2.** Sauce each plate with three pools of Burgundy Butter Sauce.

BURGUNDY BUTTER SAUCE

MAKES 2 CUPS

1 cup balsamic vinegar

1⅛ cups red wine

1 shallot, cut in half

¼ cup (½ stick) cold unsalted butter,
cut into tablespoon-size pieces

½ cup (1 stick) cold lightly salted butter,
cut into tablespoon-size pieces

1. In a medium-size heavy-bottomed saucepan, combine the vinegar, wine, and shallot over medium heat and reduce to a syrupy consistency. **2.** Using a wooden spoon, incorporate the butter into the sauce one piece at a time. When all the butter is incorporated, remove the shallot pieces. Keep warm until ready to serve.

PAN-SEARED ARCTIC CHAR ON RATATOUILLE WITH BABY SHRIMP AND ROASTED GARLIC BUTTER SAUCE

Arctic char seems to be replacing salmon in popularity on restaurant menus now that salmon is so readily available to the home cook. We find char to be a bit less fatty and more delicately flavored than salmon for this dish, but either fish may be used. The mélange of healthy garden vegetables in the ratatouille creates a nice balance with the rich and sensual roasted garlic butter sauce. You may omit the shrimp if you wish — they are simply a garnish to help keep the palate intrigued.

SERVES 6

TO MAKE THE RATATOUILLE: **1.** Film a 10-inch sauté pan with olive oil and place over medium heat. Cook the onion until wilted and translucent. Stir in the garlic, thyme, rosemary, and basil and cook 3 minutes. Remove and place in a large stainless steel mixing bowl. **2.** Heat the same sauté pan and film with oil again. Sauté the red and green peppers over high heat for several minutes, then add the zucchini and sauté over high heat until the vegetables are wilted but still crisp. Remove and add the vegetables to the mixing bowl with the onion. **3.** Heat the sauté pan and film with oil again. Over medium-high heat, quickly sauté the eggplant about 1 to 2 minutes, until lightly browned. Remove and add to the other vegetables. **4.** Pour the tomatoes onto the vegetable mixture and stir with a wooden spoon to combine. Season with salt and freshly ground pepper. **5.** Place the entire vegetable mixture in a large, heavy-bottomed pot or casserole and simmer together for 15 to 20 minutes, stirring occasionally to avoid scorching and to keep the vegetables from sticking to the bottom of the pan. **6.** Remove from the heat, check the seasonings, and rewarm just before serving. (The ratatouille may be prepared ahead to this point and kept refrigerated until needed. The flavor actually improves if the mixture rests several hours.)

TO ROAST THE GARLIC: **1.** Preheat oven to 350 degrees. **2.** Coat the unpeeled garlic with olive oil and place in a small pan. Roast at 350 degrees for about 10 to 15 minutes, until soft. **3.** Remove the head of garlic from the oven, cool slightly, and slice off the base. Gently squeeze the softened cloves out of the husk and mince. Set aside.

TO MAKE THE SAUCE: **1.** Place the wine, vinegar, and 1 tablespoon of the minced roast garlic in a 2-quart saucepan. Bring to a boil over high heat and reduce to ¼ cup. **2.** Over low heat, whisk in the cold butter 1 tablespoon at a time until all the butter is incorporated. Add the salt. **3.** Strain (optional). (The sauce may be made several hours in advance and kept warm in a double boiler off the heat.)

COOKING THE CHAR: **1.** Preheat oven to 375 degrees. **2.** Season the fish fillets with salt and white pepper. **3.** Film a 12-inch sauté pan with olive oil and heat until almost smoking. Sear the char fillets on both sides and place the pan in the

---

Six 4-ounce fillets of char
Salt and white pepper to taste
2 tablespoons olive oil

RATATOUILLE
¼ cup olive oil
1 large onion, coarsely chopped
2 tablespoons minced garlic
1 teaspoon fresh thyme leaves, minced
½ teaspoon fresh rosemary leaves, minced
6 to 8 fresh basil leaves, chopped, or
½ teaspoon dried basil
1 red bell pepper, cut into 1-inch dice
1 green bell pepper, cut into 1-inch dice
½ pound zucchini, cut into 1-inch dice
½ pound eggplant, peeled and
cut into 1-inch dice
1 pound tomatoes (or 1½ cups canned),
peeled, seeded, and diced
Salt and freshly ground pepper to taste

ROASTED GARLIC BUTTER SAUCE
½ head garlic (containing about
6 cloves), skin left on
1 tablespoon olive oil
1 cup white wine
1 cup white wine vinegar
1 pound unsalted butter, cut into
tablespoons and chilled
½ teaspoon salt

SHRIMP GARNISH
2 tablespoons olive oil
15 fresh raw baby shrimp,
peeled and cut in half
1 teaspoon minced shallot
Salt and white pepper to taste

GARNISHES
¼ cup black niçoise olives,
pitted and finely chopped
6 sprigs of dill or tarragon

4 fresh rockfish fillets, about 1½ inches
thick and 5 ounces each, skin removed

Salt and freshly ground pepper to taste

2 to 3 tablespoons olive oil

1 tablespoon cold unsalted butter

1 tablespoon pitted and finely chopped
black olives, preferably niçoise

BRAISING LIQUID

2 tablespoons olive oil

1 tablespoon minced shallot

1 teaspoon minced garlic

1 tablespoon minced celery leaves

1 teaspoon minced fresh tarragon

1 bay leaf

1 tablespoon fennel seed

1 tablespoon capers, drained

½ cup peeled, seeded, and diced
fresh tomato

2 cups dry white wine

2 cups chicken stock, preferably
homemade (see page 170)

2- to 3-inch strip orange zest

COUSCOUS

3 cups water

2 tablespoons olive oil

1 tablespoon minced shallot

2 cups Lebanese toasted couscous

2 tablespoons chopped fresh parsley

1 orange, peeled and sectioned

2 tablespoons extra-virgin olive oil

Salt and freshly ground pepper to taste

oven for 4 to 5 minutes or until the fish is just barely cooked through. Remove the fish from the pan and keep hot.

COOKING THE SHRIMP GARNISH: Film a 10-inch sauté pan with olive oil and heat until almost smoking. Add the shrimp to the pan and quickly sauté for several minutes until bright pink. Add the shallot and cook 1 minute. Season with salt and white pepper.

TO SERVE: 1. Place a large spoonful of ratatouille in the center of each of six hot serving plates. 2. Place the cooked char fillets on top of the ratatouille. 3. Ladle the roasted garlic butter sauce around the fillets. 4. Arrange the shrimp on the sauce around the perimeter of each plate. 5. Place a teaspoon of minced black olive on top of each of the fillets and garnish each with a sprig of dill or tarragon.

ROCKFISH ROASTED WITH WHITE WINE, TOMATOES, AND BLACK OLIVES ON TOASTED COUSCOUS

This is a light but lusty treatment for any white-fleshed, thick-cut fish fillet. The special Lebanese couscous is a peppercorn-size pasta with a wonderful texture, but almost any rice or pasta may be used under the fish instead. Be sure to serve with a spoon because your guests will want to finish every drop of the full-flavored aromatic broth the fish is "roasted" in.

SERVES 4

TO MAKE THE BRAISING LIQUID: 1. Preheat the oven to 400 degrees. 2. Film a 2-quart saucepan with 2 tablespoons oil. Over medium heat, sweat the shallot, garlic, celery leaves, tarragon, bay leaf, fennel, capers, and tomato for about 3 minutes. 3. Add the wine, stock, and orange zest. Simmer for 10 minutes. (The braising liquid may be prepared up to this point and stored in the refrigerator for several days. Bring to a simmer before using.)

TO COOK THE FISH: 1. Heat a 12-inch high-sided skillet or sauté pan almost to smoking. Film the pan with 2 to 3 tablespoons oil and carefully lay the rockfish fillets top side down in the pan. Sauté for 1 to 2 minutes, or until golden brown. Turn the fillets over and carefully ladle the hot braising liquid into the skillet. Bring to a boil. 2. Place the skillet on the lowest rack of the oven and bake for about 8 minutes. Test the fish for doneness; it should be just slightly resilient to the touch. 3. Remove the skillet from the oven and, using a slotted spatula, lift the fillets out of the pan. Transfer to a warm plate. 4. Place the skillet over high heat and reduce the braising liquids by one-half. Remove from the heat and stir in the butter and olives.

TO PREPARE THE COUSCOUS: 1. In a medium-size saucepan, bring the water to a rapid boil. 2. In a separate 2-quart saucepan, heat the oil over medium

heat. Add the shallot and sweat for 5 minutes. Stirring constantly, add the couscous, parsley, and orange sections.   3. Pour the boiling water over the couscous mixture. Turn the heat to high and cook for 3 minutes.   4. Drain the couscous. Dress with extra-virgin olive oil and season with salt and pepper.

TO SERVE: Place a mound of couscous on each of four deep serving plates. Lay a fish fillet on each mound and ladle the sauce over the fish.

ROCKFISH FILLETS WITH FOREST MUSHROOMS, RUBY GRAPES, AND PINE NUTS ON WILD RICE PILAF

This is a delightfully light and healthy preparation for fish fillets when fresh wild mushrooms are available. A reduction of balsamic vinegar and a sprinkling of good olive oil create the only sauce. The pine nuts and red grapes enhance the woodsy flavor of the mushrooms, making for a happy marriage of the forest, sea, and vineyard.

The wild rice pilaf may be omitted, or plain white rice may be substituted. The balsamic vinegar reduction may be made days in advance and kept handy in a squirt bottle. Any firm-fleshed white fish fillet may be used in place of the rockfish.

SERVES 4

TO MAKE THE SAUCE: In a small saucepan, combine the balsamic and red wine vinegars over medium heat. Reduce to the consistency of maple syrup. Set aside until ready to serve.

TO PREPARE THE WILD RICE PILAF: Lightly toast the pecans in a dry sauté pan over medium heat. Add the butter, wild rice, carrot, celery, and mushrooms. Sauté over medium-high heat for about 2 minutes, or until the vegetables are just tender. Season with salt and pepper.

TO SAUTÉ THE MUSHROOMS: 1. Heat the oil in a large sauté pan over high heat. Add the mushrooms and sauté for 3 to 4 minutes. Then add the shallot and garlic and sauté for 1 minute more, being careful not to burn the garlic. 2. Season with salt and pepper. Add the grapes and pine nuts, stirring lightly to combine. Set aside and keep warm.

TO COOK THE ROCKFISH: 1. Season the fillets with salt and white pepper. 2. Heat an 8-inch skillet almost to smoking and film with the oil. Sauté the fillets for about 2 minutes on each side.

TO SERVE: 1. Drizzle each of four hot serving plates with the balsamic sauce in a decorative design.   2. Mound ½ cup of wild rice pilaf on each plate. Place a rockfish fillet on top of the rice.   3. Distribute the mushroom sauté over the fish. Dribble a generous amount of olive oil over the sauté and around the plate. 4. Tuck the arugula, radicchio, or watercress leaves around and under the fish. Sprinkle with the chives.

---

4 fresh rockfish fillets, about 6 ounces each
Salt and white pepper to taste
3 tablespoons vegetable oil

BALSAMIC SAUCE
2 cups balsamic vinegar
2 cups red wine vinegar

WILD RICE PILAF
½ cup chopped pecans
2 tablespoons butter
2 cups cooked wild rice, drained
½ cup minced carrot
½ cup minced celery
½ cup minced wild mushrooms
Salt and freshly ground pepper to taste

MUSHROOM SAUTÉ
¼ cup olive oil
2 cups assorted wild mushrooms, such as shiitakes, chanterelles, or oyster mushrooms
2 teaspoons minced shallot
2 pinches minced garlic
Salt and freshly ground pepper to taste
24 red grapes, peeled
¼ cup pine nuts, toasted

GARNISHES
Extra-virgin olive oil
Fresh arugula, radicchio, or watercress leaves
1 tablespoon chopped fresh chives

2 eggs
1 tablespoon cold water
Salt and white pepper to taste
2 tablespoons unsalted butter
1 tablespoon chopped shallot
2 to 3 ounces cooked lobster meat, coarsely chopped
2 tablespoons grated white cheddar cheese
Rainbow Salsa (recipe follows)
1 tablespoon chopped fresh chives

LOBSTER OMELETTE WITH RAINBOW SALSA

GQ *magazine awarded us its Golden Dish Award for this omelette, naming it "one of the ten best restaurant dishes in the world." If you have a bit of leftover lobster in the house, nothing could be simpler. Crabmeat or baby shrimp may be substituted for the lobster. This omelette is ideal as a quick brunch or supper dish.*

SERVES 1

1. In a small stainless steel bowl, whisk together the eggs, water, salt, and white pepper. 2. In a small sauté pan, melt 1 tablespoon of the butter over medium heat. Add the shallot and lobster and season with salt and white pepper, heating just until warm. Set aside and keep warm. 3. In a 7-inch omelette pan, melt the remaining 1 tablespoon butter over high heat. As the butter melts, tilt the pan, allowing the butter to film the sides. When the butter foams and is on the verge of turning brown, quickly pour in the egg mixture, stirring vigorously with a fork until the eggs are scrambled into a broken custard. 4. Stop stirring and, using a rubber spatula, gently loosen the omelette from the pan. Sprinkle half the cheese in a line near the center of the eggs perpendicular to the handle of the pan. Top the cheese with the warm lobster mixture and cover with the remaining cheese. 5. Tilt the pan at a 45-degree angle, allowing the edge of the omelette to slide down onto the lip of the pan and fold back over the filling. Using a rubber spatula, fold the other edge of the omelette over the filling. Holding a warm plate in your left hand, flip the omelette onto the plate, seam side down. 6. Gently warm the Rainbow Salsa in a small saucepan.

TO SERVE: Spoon 2 tablespoons of the warm salsa in a ribbon over the omelette and sprinkle with the chives.

NOTE: For the most comprehensive explanation of how to make a French-style rolled or folded omelette, read Julia Child's *Mastering the Art of French Cooking,* volume I, page 126. Most Americans do not understand that an omelette is, by definition, scrambled eggs encased in an envelope of egg. Since this basic concept is so widely misunderstood, many cooks don't know what they're aiming for. Consequently, a correctly cooked omelette is close to impossible to find in the United States.

¼ cup diced red bell pepper
¼ cup diced yellow bell pepper
¼ cup diced green bell pepper
¼ cup diced red onion
1 teaspoon balsamic vinegar
1 teaspoon extra-virgin olive oil
Salt and freshly ground pepper to taste

RAINBOW SALSA

MAKES 1 CUP

Combine all the ingredients in a small bowl. Cover and refrigerate until ready to use.

6

SIDE DISHES

CREAMY GARLIC POLENTA

This polenta is addictive, easy to make, and incredibly versatile. It can be used as a side dish or chilled, cut into pieces, and fried in olive oil as an accompaniment to anything from fish to foie gras.

SERVES 6

1 tablespoon unsalted butter

1 tablespoon olive oil

1 teaspoon minced garlic

1½ cups heavy cream

1½ cups milk

1½ cups water

⅛ teaspoon cayenne pepper

1 bay leaf

½ cup yellow cornmeal

½ cup grated Asiago or Parmesan cheese

1. In a 2-quart heavy-bottomed saucepan, melt the butter over medium heat. Add the oil and garlic. Sweat the garlic for about 2 minutes, but don't let it brown. **2.** Add the cream, milk, and water to the pan and increase the heat to high. Add the cayenne pepper and bay leaf. Let simmer for 5 minutes, then remove the bay leaf. **3.** Whisking constantly, pour the cornmeal into the boiling liquid in a thin stream. Cook, stirring constantly with a wooden spoon, until the polenta begins to thicken. Stir in the cheese. **4.** Pour the polenta out into a jelly-roll pan and keep warm until ready to serve.

TO SERVE: The polenta may be scooped warm onto serving plates or chilled, cut into shapes, and fried in olive oil.

*1½ pounds very thin French green beans
(haricots verts)*

1 tablespoon unsalted butter

1 rounded teaspoon chopped shallot

¼ teaspoon minced garlic

Pinch of sugar

*¼ teaspoon chopped fresh tarragon
or marjoram*

Salt and freshly ground pepper to taste

¼ cup Brown Butter (see page 169)

SAUTÉED FRESH GREEN BEANS

SERVES 6

1. Trim the ends from the beans and wash thoroughly. **2.** Bring a 6-quart pot of salted water to a rolling boil. Drop in the beans and cook for 4 minutes. **3.** Remove the beans and immediately plunge into a bowl of ice water for 2 to 3 minutes. Drain and thoroughly dry. **4.** In a 10-inch sauté pan, melt the butter over medium heat, moving it around the pan so that it leaves a thin film over the entire surface. When the butter begins to brown, add the beans and sauté for 1½ minutes over high heat. Constantly toss or lift the beans with a big spoon to prevent burning. **5.** Add the shallot and garlic and sauté for about 1 minute, continuing to move the ingredients around the pan. **6.** Add the sugar, tarragon or marjoram, and salt and pepper. Stir briefly, about 10 seconds. Pour the Brown Butter over the beans, stir once, and remove from the heat.

NOTE: The entire cooking time in the sauté pan should not exceed 3 minutes.

OVEN-ROASTED PLUM TOMATOES

Here is a solution for the scarcity of delicious-tasting fresh tomatoes during the winter. Little plum tomatoes (usually available year-round) are coated with olive oil and salt and roasted in a low oven. They can be stored for a week or so in olive oil in the refrigerator. Simply slip off the skin before using.

Oven-roasted tomatoes make an economical alternative to expensive sun-dried tomatoes and are far more versatile. They're surprisingly good on salads and in stir-fried dishes, and sensational on sandwiches, especially grilled cheese.

6 fresh Italian plum or Roma tomatoes

¼ cup olive oil

1 tablespoon kosher salt

6 fresh basil leaves (optional)

MAKES 6 TOMATOES

1. Preheat the oven to 200 degrees. **2.** Using a sharp-tipped paring knife, core the tomatoes. Place in a small bowl and toss with the oil and salt. If desired, stuff a basil leaf into the center of each tomato. **3.** Lay the tomatoes on a rack in a small roasting pan and bake for about 4 hours, or until the skins crack and blister. The tomatoes should have a slightly charred appearance.

TO SERVE: Cool the tomatoes, then remove the basil leaves. Peel, quarter, or halve the tomatoes and use as you would fresh ones.

TO STORE: Pack the tomatoes closely in a jar or plastic container and cover with extra-virgin olive oil. Herbs and garlic may be added to the oil to enhance the flavor.

1 pound dried Great Northern beans
1 tablespoon salt
1 cup sugar
3 strips bacon, cut into ½-inch pieces
2 tablespoons butter

MY GRANDMOTHER'S BAKED BEANS

I grew up eating these beans at picnics and family gatherings. Everyone always raved about them. When I finally asked my mother for the recipe, I was shocked at the amount of sugar in the ingredients and thought it must be a mistake. Little did I know that sugar was Granny's little secret. Think of them as caramelized baked beans. They're best baked and served in an earthenware crock, and you'll be amazed at how deliciously old-timey they taste, either hot or at room temperature. They can be made long in advance of serving.

SERVES 4

1. Place the beans in a 2-quart saucepan and cover with cool water. Soak overnight. **2.** Drain the beans, cover with fresh salted water, and cook over medium heat until just barely tender. **3.** Preheat the oven to 300 degrees. **4.** Stir the sugar and bacon into the beans and place, along with the cooking water, in an ovenproof earthenware crock or bean pot. Top with the butter and bake, uncovered, in a pre-heated 300 degree oven for 3 hours. If the top layer of beans begins to burn or becomes too dry, cover the pot with aluminum foil.

1 quart vegetable oil
4 parsnips, peeled
Salt to taste

PARSNIP CRISPS

These curly parsnip crisps make a relatively quick and easy cocktail tidbit or can be used as a garnish for soups or main courses in need of a little dramatic flair.

50 TO 60 CRISPS

1. In a 4-quart saucepan, heat the vegetable oil to approximately 350 degrees. **2.** Lay each parsnip on a flat surface and, using a vegetable peeler, slice it lengthwise into thin ribbons. **3.** Drop the parsnip ribbons into the hot oil and gently swirl them with a wooden spoon until the edges begin to turn golden brown, about 30 seconds. **4.** Using a Chinese dipper or slotted spoon, remove the crisps from the oil and drain on paper towels. Sprinkle with salt. The crisps will hold for several days in an airtight container.

SILVER QUEEN CORN SAUTÉ

This is one of our favorite ways to use fresh sweet corn. It's a wonderful vegetable dish on its own, but we also use it in combination with various grilled and sautéed fish dishes, under soft-shell crabs, and with lobster, beef, and veal. Blanching the bacon gives it a much more subtle flavor, preventing the smokiness from overwhelming the more delicate taste of the corn.

SERVES 6

1. Shuck the corn, brushing off all the silk. Strip the kernels off the ears with a sharp knife. **2.** In a 2-quart saucepan, blanch the bacon in boiling water for 1 minute. Drain and dry on a paper towel. **3.** Place the bacon in a sauté pan and cook until crisp and brown. Using a slotted spoon, remove the bacon and pour off half the fat from the pan. **4.** Add the red and green bell peppers to the pan and sweat over medium heat for about 2 minutes. Add the corn and sauté for 3 to 4 minutes more. **5.** Add the balsamic vinegar, sugar, and salt and pepper. Return the bacon to the pan and add the cilantro. **6.** Remove the corn mixture from the pan and keep warm until ready to serve.

*6 ears fresh sweet corn
(approximately 5 to 6 cups kernels)
4 strips bacon, diced
1 red bell pepper, finely diced
1 green bell pepper, finely diced
1 tablespoon balsamic vinegar
1 tablespoon sugar
Salt and freshly ground pepper to taste
1½ tablespoons chopped fresh cilantro*

½ head savoy cabbage

1 strip thick bacon or 2 strips thin, diced

½ large red onion, thinly sliced

1 tablespoon mustard seeds

2 tablespoons sugar

¼ cup white wine vinegar

½ bunch watercress, coarse stems removed

Freshly ground pepper to taste

A TANGLE OF TART GREENS

This is a wonderfully simple and versatile garnish or accompaniment. We use it with duck, venison, roast pork, sausage, or even soft-shell crabs. In the winter months it can take the place of a green vegetable. The crunchy texture of the cabbage makes chewy foods seem tender.

SERVES 4

1. Core and coarsely shred the cabbage with a sharp knife or mandoline. **2.** In a 10-inch skillet, sauté the bacon over medium heat until lightly browned. Add the onion and cabbage and sauté until the cabbage begins to wilt. Add the mustard seeds, sugar, and vinegar and cook until the cabbage is tender but still crisp. **3.** Remove the skillet from the heat. Toss in the watercress and season with pepper. Serve warm.

ROASTED TOMATO AND SHALLOT FONDUE

Fondue simply means "melted," and this savory condiment is an apt illustration of the term, since the roasted tomatoes and shallots seem literally to have melted together. The fondue can be made up to a week in advance and kept in the refrigerator as a flavor enhancer for fish or steaks. It also may be used as a stuffing for portobello mushrooms (see page 00). When storing in the refrigerator, pour a thin film of olive oil on top to prevent mixture from drying out. Re-heat before serving.

SERVES 8

1. Preheat the oven to 350 degrees. 2. Lay the shallots in a small, shallow, ovenproof baking dish and pour the oil over them to a depth of ½ inch. Cover the dish with aluminum foil or a lid and bake for 1 hour, or until the shallots are soft. 3. When the shallots are cool enough to handle, peel off the skin and squeeze out the flesh. Coarsely chop the shallot flesh and the roasted tomatoes. Combine in a medium-size bowl. Add the vinegar and salt and pepper. Mix well and place in a Pyrex baking dish about 2 inches deep. Press the bay leaves and thyme sprigs into the mixture. (If using dried thyme, stir it in.) 4. Bake, uncovered, for about 15 minutes, or until slightly thickened. Stir occasionally to prevent a crust from forming. 5. Remove fondue from the oven. Discard the bay leaves and thyme sprigs.

12 whole fresh shallots, unpeeled
Olive oil
24 Oven-Roasted Plum Tomatoes (see page 108), peeled
2 tablespoons balsamic vinegar
Salt and freshly ground pepper to taste
2 bay leaves
2 sprigs fresh thyme or 1 teaspoon dried

WILD RICE PECAN PILAF

With the few little extra ingredients in this recipe, basic wild rice becomes exciting, colorful, and crunchy. The wild rice may be cooked and stored in the refrigerator up to two days before serving. It can be sautéed with the vegetables and nuts up to an hour before serving and kept warm.

SERVES 4

1. In a medium-size saucepan, bring 2 quarts of water to a rapid boil. Add the ½ teaspoon salt and wild rice. Boil, uncovered, for 40 to 45 minutes, or until the grains just begin to pop open and the rice is just tender. Drain and set aside. 2. In a 10-inch skillet, melt the butter over medium heat. Add the carrot and sauté for 1 to 2 minutes. Add the celery, mushrooms, and pecans. Sauté for about 2 minutes more, stirring often. Add the rice and sauté until thoroughly combined. Season with salt and pepper.

½ teaspoon salt
¾ cup wild rice
2 tablespoons butter
1 medium-size carrot, peeled and minced
1 stalk celery, minced
½ cup white mushrooms, minced
½ cup toasted pecans, coarsely chopped
Salt and freshly ground pepper to taste

GARLIC PUREE

12 cloves garlic, unpeeled

½ cup olive oil

1 cup chicken stock, preferably
homemade (see page 170)

1 cup heavy cream

CUSTARD

4 whole eggs

2 egg yolks

1 cup heavy cream

Pinch of sugar

Salt and white pepper to taste

Nonstick cooking spray

GARLIC CUSTARD

These savory, golden yellow custards are a sensuous accompaniment to a roast leg or rack of lamb or a platter of sliced meat. They also can be used as an elegant garnish for a clear chicken soup or consommé. Simply unmold them, place one in the center of each soup plate, and ladle the broth around it.

SERVES 10

TO MAKE THE GARLIC PUREE: 1. Preheat the oven to 350 degrees. 2. Place the garlic in a small, ovenproof baking dish and cover with the oil. Bake, uncovered, for 25 minutes. 3. Remove the pan from the oven and carefully strain the garlic, reserving the oil for another use. When the garlic cloves are cool enough to handle, squeeze out the flesh, discarding the papery outer skin. 4. Place the roasted garlic in a 2-quart saucepan and add the stock and cream. Cook over medium heat until liquid has reduced to about 1 cup. 5. Puree the mixture in a blender or food processor and strain. Cool to room temperature. (The garlic puree may be prepared a day in advance and kept refrigerated.)

TO MAKE THE CUSTARD: 1. Preheat the oven to 350 degrees. 2. In a large bowl, whisk the eggs and yolks together. Whisk in the cream and garlic puree. Add the sugar and season with salt and white pepper. 3. Coat the insides of ten 5-ounce metal timbale molds or ceramic or glass custard molds with nonstick cooking spray and fill each halfway with custard. 4. Set the filled molds in a shallow baking pan and carefully place on a rack in the lower third of the oven. Pour very hot water to a depth of 1 inch around the molds and bake for 35 to 40 minutes, or until the custard is just set. 5. Remove the custards from the water bath and cool slightly. If you're not ready to serve them, the custards may be kept warm in their molds in the water bath.

TO SERVE: Run the tip of a sharp knife around the edge of each custard and unmold onto a platter or individual serving plates.

½ medium-size onion, thinly sliced
4 Idaho potatoes
1 tablespoon butter
3 cups heavy cream
Pinch of freshly grated nutmeg
Salt and freshly ground pepper to taste

POTATOES BAKED IN CREAM

We've been serving this heavenly version of scalloped potatoes in individual casseroles since the day The Inn opened. Low cal they're not, however once you've tried them, you'll never bother with ordinary scalloped potatoes again. Servings should be small. Be sure not to lay the potatoes too thickly in the baking dishes.

The wonderful thing about this method is that you can partially cook the potatoes and onions in cream on top of the stove ahead of time — even the day before — then spoon them into ovenproof gratin dishes or casseroles and finish in the oven 15 minutes before you're ready to serve. Turnips or carrots can be cooked in exactly the same way, or you can mix turnips, carrots, and potatoes together. During black truffle season, we layer thin slices of fresh truffle between the layers of potatoes and reminisce about Henry VIII.

SERVES 6 TO 8

1. Peel the onion and slice as thinly as possible. Peel the potatoes and slice as evenly as possible about ⅛ inch thick.   2. In a 4-quart heavy-bottomed saucepan, melt the butter over medium heat. Add the onion slices. Stir with a wooden spoon and cook until the onions are wilted and translucent.   3. Add the cream and bring to a boil. Add the potatoes, folding them into the cream with a rubber spatula to make sure each slice is well coated. Add the nutmeg and season with salt and pepper. 4. Simmer until the cream begins to thicken and the potatoes are almost tender. They should still have some resistance to the bite. (The recipe can be completed up to this stage well in advance. If you are not ready to proceed with serving the potatoes, remove them from the pan and store in a covered container in the refrigerator.)   5. Preheat the oven to 375 degrees.   6. In six to eight shallow, ovenproof gratin dishes or individual casseroles or in one large Pyrex baking dish, spoon a layer of the potatoes and cream mixture about 1 inch deep. (It's not necessary to grease the dishes first.) The casseroles can be assembled to this point well in advance of baking. The potatoes will not discolor since they are already partially cooked.   7. Bake in the upper third of the oven at 375 degrees for 12 to 15 minutes, or until the tip of a paring knife slides easily into the potatoes and they are golden brown on top.

SPAETZLE

Spaetzle, *which means "little sparrows" in German, undoubtedly takes its name from the amusing and irregular shapes that these boiled egg dumplings take on when they fall into boiling water. They're irresistible sautéed in butter with a sprinkling of freshly grated nutmeg.*

SERVES 4

3½ cups all-purpose flour
1 teaspoon salt
3 whole eggs
2 egg yolks
1 cup water
Olive oil
3 tablespoons butter
Pinch of freshly grated nutmeg
Salt and freshly ground pepper to taste
1 teaspoon chopped fresh parsley

1. Sift the flour and salt into a large bowl and form a well in the center. Place the eggs, yolks, and water in the well and mix with a wooden spoon until well blended and smooth.   2. In a large pot, bring 4 quarts of salted water to a rapid boil. Using a cheese grater or metal colander, push and scrape the dough across the colander openings, letting the little "teardrops" of dough fall into the boiling water about 1 cup at a time. Boil the spaetzle for 1 minute. Using a mesh strainer, dip the spaetzle out of the pot and plunge it into a bowl of ice water to stop the cooking. Continue in this manner until all the dough is cooked and chilled. Drain the spaetzle and sprinkle with olive oil.

TO SAUTÉ THE SPAETZLE: 1. In a large sauté pan, melt the butter over medium heat until it begins to take on color. Immediately add the spaetzle and sauté until each little dumpling is well coated with butter and slightly crisp. Sprinkle with the nutmeg and salt and pepper.   2. Remove from the heat and sprinkle with parsley.

GARLIC MASHED POTATOES

Adding roasted garlic to a basic potato puree adds a whole new dimension to the mashed potatoes we grew up eating.

SERVES 6

10 cloves garlic
1 teaspoon olive oil
4 large Idaho potatoes, peeled and quartered
⅔ cup heavy cream
½ cup crème fraîche or sour cream
6 tablespoons butter
Pinch of cayenne pepper
Salt and white pepper to taste

1. Preheat the oven to 350 degrees.   2. Toss the garlic in the oil and wrap in aluminum foil. Roast for 25 minutes. Remove from the oven and allow to cool to room temperature.   3. Place the potatoes in a large pot and cover with cold water. Bring to a gentle boil.   4. While the potatoes are cooking, peel the garlic and mash it in a mortar and pestle or with a fork in a small bowl.   5. In a small saucepan over medium heat, warm the cream, crème fraîche or sour cream, butter, and mashed garlic.   6. When the potatoes are tender, drain and place them in the bowl of an electric mixer fitted with the paddle attachment. Whip until smooth and fluffy. While whipping, slowly pour the warm cream mixture into the potatoes until thoroughly incorporated. Add the cayenne and season with salt and white pepper.

7

DESSERTS

COEUR À LA CRÈME
WITH RASPBERRY SAUCE

Coeur à la crème is an old French country concoction that is both earthy and elegant, rustic and dressy—appropriate for any occasion. It's a wonderful complement to whatever summer berries are in season. This dessert is served at The Inn to celebrate birthdays and anniversaries. It can be made in less than five minutes and never fails to knock 'em out—even more so than an elaborate cake that took two days to execute.

One large (16-ounce) or four individual (4-ounce) perforated heart-shaped ceramic molds lined with cheesecloth will be needed to create this dessert. The perforated molds allow the excess liquid, or whey, to drip through the cheesecloth, leaving the delicious "heart" of the cream. Coeur à la crème molds are usually available at kitchen supply stores.

SERVES 4

1. Cut a piece of cheesecloth into four 6-inch squares. Dampen and wring out lightly. Press one square into each of four perforated heart-shaped ceramic molds and set aside.   2. In the bowl of an electric mixer, whip the mascarpone cheese, ¼ cup of the cream, the vanilla, the 1 tablespoon lemon juice, and the Chambord until thoroughly blended. Refrigerate.   3. In a small bowl, whip the remaining 1 cup cream and the confectioners' sugar until the cream forms stiff peaks.   4. With a rubber spatula, fold the whipped cream into the chilled cheese mixture in three batches.   5. Spoon the finished mixture into the prepared molds and fold the edges of the cheesecloth over the tops. Lightly tap the bottoms of the molds on the counter to remove any air spaces between the mixture and the molds. Refrigerate on a tray or baking sheet a minimum of 2 to 3 hours.

RASPBERRY SAUCE: In a blender or food processor, puree the raspberries, granulated sugar, and 1 teaspoon lemon juice. Taste the sauce for sweetness and adjust the sugar or lemon juice as needed. Strain and refrigerate.

TO SERVE: 1. Unfold the cheesecloth and drape it over the sides of the molds. Invert each mold onto a serving plate. While pressing down on the corners of the cheesecloth, carefully lift off the mold. Smooth the top with the back of a spoon and remove the cheesecloth slowly.   2. Spoon raspberry sauce onto the plate around the heart and garnish with fresh berries and mint leaves.

8 ounces mascarpone cheese, softened
1¼ cups heavy cream
1 teaspoon vanilla extract
1 tablespoon fresh lemon juice
1 tablespoon Chambord or other raspberry liqueur
½ cup sifted confectioners' sugar

RASPBERRY SAUCE
1 pint fresh raspberries
1 tablespoon granulated sugar
1 teaspoon fresh lemon juice

GARNISHES
Fresh raspberries
Mint leaves

Basic Pie Dough (see page 157)
2 Granny Smith apples
3 tablespoons unsalted butter
½ teaspoon ground cinnamon
2 tablespoons heavy cream
6 tablespoons Southern Comfort
Nonstick cooking spray
⅓ cup sugar combined with 1 rounded
teaspoon ground cinnamon
Vanilla Ice Cream (see page 154)
or crème fraîche

WARM GRANNY SMITH APPLE TART

Being in the heart of apple-growing country, we've tried every apple dessert imaginable over the years. This is the most delicate of apple tarts. Apple slices are sautéed briefly in butter, whiskey, and cream, then arranged on thin disks of pastry and baked just before serving. A scoop of ice cream melting on top makes them even more irresistible. The tarts can be assembled well in advance and baked just before serving. Croissant dough or puff pastry may be substituted for the pie dough.

SERVES 6

1. On a floured board, roll the dough out to about ⅛ inch thick. Lay a bowl about 5 inches in diameter upside down on the dough and, using the rim as a pattern, cut out six circles with a sharp paring knife. Place the pastry rounds between sheets of waxed paper and refrigerate. **2.** Peel and core the apples. Using a mandoline or sharp knife, slice the apples into ⅛-inch sections. **3.** In a large sauté pan, melt the butter over medium heat. Add the apples and cook for several minutes. Add the cinnamon and cream. Carefully add the Southern Comfort, averting your face, as it will ignite. Continue cooking until the apples are soft and pliable. **4.** Remove the apples with a slotted spoon and place on a nonreactive baking sheet. Cool in the refrigerator. **5.** Simmer the cooking liquid until reduced by one-half. Set this mixture aside to glaze the tarts after they have baked. **6.** Remove the pastry rounds from the refrigerator. Spray several baking sheets with nonstick cooking spray and lay the rounds on them. Place the chilled apple slices in concentric circles around the pastry, leaving a ¼-inch border at the edges. Roll one apple slice into a tight circle to form a rosette and place in the center of each tart. (The tarts may be assembled up to this point and refrigerated.) **7.** Preheat the oven to 400 degrees. **8.** Dust the tarts with cinnamon sugar and bake for about 7 minutes, or until the crust is a rich golden brown. **9.** Remove the tarts from the oven and brush with the reserved cooking liquid.

TO SERVE: Serve the tarts on individual plates with a scoop of Vanilla Ice Cream or a dollop of crème fraîche.

APPLE-WALNUT ROSE

This is a fragile, apple-filled, warm phyllo pastry in the shape of a rose sauced with sour cream and caramel sauces. The pastry can be completely assembled well in advance, refrigerated, and baked just before serving. The presentation is so striking that your guests will think you studied pastry making in Austria.

SERVES 8

1. Preheat the oven to 350 degrees.   2. Peel the apples, cut them in half, and remove the cores. Lay the apple halves flat side down in a small baking dish.
3. Pour the rum and lemon juice over the apples and sprinkle with the sugar, cinnamon, and cloves. Cover with aluminum foil and bake for 20 to 25 minutes, or until the point of a sharp knife slides easily into the apples.   4. Remove the apples from the oven and let cool.   5. Roughly chop the cooled apples. Place in a medium-size bowl with the Walnut Cream and chopped walnuts.   6. Lay one sheet of phyllo pastry out on a work surface and cut it into four equal squares. Brush each square with melted butter.   7. Place about ½ cup of the apple filling on one of the squares and gather up the edges around the filling, making a pouch. Pinch the edges of the pastry to seal the filling. Lay the pouch on top of the another square and draw up the edges loosely, twisting slightly to form a petal shape. Continue wrapping, using the remaining two squares. Repeat this process for the remaining seven roses.
8. Brush the bottom of each rose with melted butter. Place on a baking sheet and refrigerate for at least 15 minutes.   9. Preheat the oven to 375 degrees.   10. Bake the roses for 10 minutes, or until the edges are crisp and golden brown. Remove the pastries from the oven and dust with confectioners' sugar.

TO SERVE: Using a spatula, lift each rose onto a warm serving plate and ladle the Sour Cream Sauce around it. Drizzle the Caramel Sauce on top of the sour cream and swirl the sauces together with a knife. Serve the roses warm.

WALNUT CREAM

MAKES 2 CUPS

1. In a medium-size bowl, cream the sugar and butter together until light and fluffy.
2. Add the flour, eggs, walnuts, rum, vanilla, cinnamon, nutmeg, and lemon juice. Mix well. Chill in the refrigerator.

SOUR CREAM SAUCE

MAKES 2 ⅓ CUPS

In a small bowl, whisk together the sour cream, confectioners' sugar, vanilla, and lemon juice. Store in the refrigerator until ready to use.

---

4 Granny Smith apples
¼ cup dark rum
2 tablespoons fresh lemon juice
2 tablespoons sugar
1 teaspoon ground cinnamon
¼ teaspoon ground cloves
Walnut Cream (recipe follows)
½ cup coarsely chopped walnuts
1 package (1 pound) phyllo pastry
6 tablespoons butter, melted
½ cup confectioners' sugar
(for dusting pastries)
Sour Cream Sauce (recipe follows)
Caramel Sauce (recipe follows)

⅔ cup sugar
½ cup (1 stick) butter, softened
2 tablespoons flour
2 eggs
1½ cups walnuts, coarsely chopped
2 tablespoons dark rum
1 teaspoon vanilla extract
Ground cinnamon and nutmeg to taste
Fresh lemon juice to taste

2 cups sour cream
⅓ cup sifted confectioners' sugar
1 teaspoon vanilla extract
½ teaspoon fresh lemon juice

1½ cups sugar
½ cup water
1 cup heavy cream
½ cup (1 stick) butter

CRUST
2½ cups ground pecans
(about 12 ounces whole pecans)
⅓ cup sugar
¼ cup (½ stick) unsalted butter, melted
2 ounces semisweet chocolate, melted

GRAPEFRUIT CUSTARD FILLING
¼ cup (½ stick) unsalted butter
¾ cup sugar
½ cup heavy cream
⅔ cup fresh grapefruit juice
½ cup fresh orange juice
4 eggs, lightly beaten
Grated zest of 1 grapefruit
2 teaspoons unflavored gelatin

GARNISHES
Whipped cream
Grapefruit sections

CARAMEL SAUCE

MAKES 2¼ CUPS

1. In a large saucepan, caramelize the sugar and water. Remove from heat.
2. Heat the cream and slowly whisk into the caramel. Be careful of rising steam.
3. Whisk in small pieces of softened butter. Cool.

GRAPEFRUIT TART WITH CHOCOLATE-PECAN CRUST

This custard tart is at once startling and refreshing. The chocolate may be eliminated if you wish, and any other nut may be substituted for the pecans in the crust.

SERVES 8

TO MAKE THE CRUST: 1. In a small bowl, combine the pecans, sugar, and melted butter. Pat into a 9-inch Pyrex pie dish. Chill for 30 minutes in the refrigerator. 2. Preheat the oven to 375 degrees. 3. Bake the pecan crust for 10 minutes. Set aside to cool to room temperature. 4. Using a pastry brush, spread the melted chocolate over the inside of the crust and set aside.

TO MAKE THE FILLING: 1. In a 2-quart saucepan, melt the butter over medium heat. Add the sugar and stir until dissolved. 2. Add the cream, ½ cup of the grapefruit juice, the orange juice, eggs, and grapefruit zest. Sprinkle the gelatin over the remaining grapefruit juice to soften and set aside. 3. Cook the cream-citrus mixture over low heat, stirring constantly, until it thickens and lightly coats the back of a spoon. Do not allow it to come to a boil, or the eggs may curdle. 4. Add the gelatin mixture and stir until the gelatin is dissolved. 5. When the custard is a cool room temperature, pour it into the chocolate-coated crust and refrigerate until set, about 2 hours.

TO SERVE: Cut the tart into wedges and garnish with the whipped cream and grapefruit sections.

Nonstick cooking spray

3 eggs, separated

¾ cup firmly packed brown sugar

½ cup pumpkin puree or canned pumpkin

¼ teaspoon peeled, minced fresh ginger (optional)

¾ cup all-purpose flour

½ teaspoon baking soda

½ teaspoon ground cinnamon

¼ teaspoon salt

¼ teaspoon ground cloves

2 tablespoons confectioners' sugar

Pumpkin Ice Cream (see page 150)

GARNISHES

1 cup pecans

2 cups heavy cream

¼ cup confectioners' sugar

4 ounces candied ginger

Crème Anglaise (see page 157)

DOUBLE-PUMPKIN ROULADE

At last, an elegant and refreshing pumpkin dessert that can be made days in advance. Perfect for a special fall dinner and the ideal solution for the Thanksgiving Day dessert dilemma. A pumpkin jelly-roll cake is rolled around pumpkin ice cream, garnished with toasted pecans and candied ginger, and sauced with a crème anglaise.

SERVES 12

1. Preheat the oven to 375 degrees. **2.** Spray a baking sheet with nonstick cooking spray. Line the sheet with parchment or waxed paper and spray again. Dust lightly with flour. **3.** In the bowl of an electric mixer, beat the egg yolks until slightly thickened, about 5 minutes, and gradually mix in the brown sugar. Stir in the pumpkin and optional ginger. **4.** Sift together the flour, baking soda, cinnamon, salt, and cloves. Fold into the egg mixture. **5.** In a separate bowl, beat the egg whites until they form stiff peaks. Using a rubber spatula, fold the whites into the batter. **6.** Pour the batter onto the prepared baking sheet and spread evenly into all four corners. Bake the cake for 10 to 12 minutes, or until just set. **7.** Run a knife around the edges of the cake to loosen it from the pan. Invert the cake onto a clean tea towel dusted with the confectioners' sugar. Peel off the parchment or waxed paper. Roll the cake up in the towel lengthwise and place in the refrigerator to cool.

TO ASSEMBLE: 1. Line the same baking sheet you used to bake the cake (or one that is identical in size) with plastic wrap. Spread the Pumpkin Ice Cream evenly onto the baking sheet and place in the freezer for about 30 minutes, or until firm. **2.** When the ice cream is firm, trim off a 2-inch strip from the edge (lengthwise). Save for another use. **3.** Remove the cake from the refrigerator and unroll. **4.** Lift the ice cream out of the pan using the plastic wrap. Invert on top of the cake with the near edge flush with the edge of the cake. Do not remove the plastic. **5.** Probe the surface of the ice cream with a finger to check for stiffness. When the ice cream softens enough to dimple under moderate pressure, it is pliable enough to roll. Quickly peel off the plastic wrap and slowly and evenly roll the cake up lengthwise around the ice cream in the form of a jelly roll. Rest the cake on its seam, wrap in foil, and freeze until ready to serve.

TO SERVE: 1. Preheat the oven to 350 degrees. **2.** Toast the pecans on a baking sheet for 3 to 4 minutes, or until they begin to color. **3.** In the bowl of an electric mixer, whip the cream with the remaining ¼ cup confectioners' sugar until it forms stiff peaks. Transfer to a pastry bag fitted with a decorative tip. **4.** Slice the candied ginger into thin strips. **5.** Using a sharp knife, slice the thoroughly frozen cake on the bias about 1½ inches thick and place on chilled serving plates. **6.** Pipe rosettes of sweetened whipped cream on top of each slice of cake and garnish with toasted pecans and candied ginger. **7.** Sauce with Crème Anglaise.

GÂTEAU DE DEUX CHOCOLATS GLACÉ (DOUBLE-CHOCOLATE ICE CREAM CAKE)

When I was growing up, it used to be a big treat to buy one of those frozen ice cream cake rolls at the dairy store. I couldn't imagine how they got the ice cream rolled inside the cake. This is the adult version of that childhood delight — a flourless chocolate cake wrapped around homemade White Chocolate Ice Cream, sauced with warm dark and white chocolate sauces, and garnished with whipped cream and chocolate curls. This is a decadent dessert. Parental guidance is advised.

SERVES 10

TO MAKE THE CAKE: 1. Line a 15½- by 10½-inch baking sheet with aluminum foil, smoothing out any wrinkles with a kitchen towel. Spray the foil with a thin coating of nonstick cooking spray. Dust with the flour, tapping the back of the pan to remove any excess flour. 2. Preheat the oven to 325 degrees. 3. Separate the eggs. Reserve the egg whites. Place the yolks and granulated sugar in the bowl of an electric mixer. Whisk until the yolks are lemon yellow and fluffy, about 5 minutes. Whisk in the melted chocolate, scraping down the sides of the bowl with a rubber spatula to incorporate thoroughly. 4. In a medium-size bowl, whisk the egg whites until they begin to foam. Add the salt and continue whisking until egg whites form stiff peaks. 5. Using a rubber spatula, gently fold the egg whites into the chocolate mixture a third at a time, being careful not to overmix. Pour the batter into the prepared pan, smoothing it into the corners with a rubber spatula. 6. Bake for 4 minutes, rotate, and bake for 4 minutes more. Remove from the oven and cool in the pan. 7. Cover the cake with plastic wrap and refrigerate in the pan until ready to proceed with rolling the cake.

TO ROLL THE CAKE AROUND THE ICE CREAM: 1. Line a 15½- by 10½-inch sheet pan (exactly the same size as the one you used to bake the cake) with plastic wrap. Working quickly, spread the White Chocolate Ice Cream over the plastic wrap about ½ inch deep. Immediately place the sheet of ice cream in the freezer and freeze until stiff, about 3 hours. 2. Loosen the cake from the pan by running a knife around the edges. Invert onto a clean tea towel dusted with the confectioners' sugar. 3. Remove the ice cream from the freezer and trim a 2-inch strip from the edge (lengthwise). Save for another use. Using the edges of the plastic wrap, lift the ice cream out of the pan and invert it on top of the cake with the near edge flush with the edge of the cake. Do not remove the plastic. Probe the surface of the ice cream with a finger to check the stiffness. When the ice cream softens enough to dimple under moderate pressure, it is pliable enough to roll. 4. Working quickly, hold the ice cream and plastic in place while lifting the cake with the edge of the towel. Curl the edge of the cake evenly from one end to the other. Remove the plastic wrap and continue rolling the cake tightly around the ice cream. Wrap the cake in aluminum foil, crimping the ends closed, and freeze overnight.

TO MAKE THE GARNISHES: 1. In the bowl of an electric mixer, whip the cream with the confectioners' sugar until it forms stiff peaks. Place in a pastry bag fitted with a decorative tip. 2. Rub one side of a slab or bar of chocolate with your

Nonstick cooking spray
1 tablespoon flour (for dusting the pan)
7 eggs
½ cup granulated sugar
8 ounces semisweet chocolate, melted
Pinch of salt
White Chocolate Ice Cream (see page 154)
¼ cup confectioners' sugar (for dusting the cake)

GARNISHES
1 cup heavy cream
¼ cup confectioners' sugar
8-ounce block semisweet chocolate for making chocolate curls
White Chocolate Sauce (see page 156), warmed
Dark Chocolate Sauce (see page 154), warmed

fingers to warm it slightly, then drag a sharp knife across it to make chocolate curl garnishes. Keep the curls in the freezer until ready to use.

TO SERVE: 1. Using a sharp knife, slice the thoroughly frozen cake on the bias about 1½ inches thick. Place one slice on each of ten chilled serving plates. **2.** Pipe rosettes of sweetened whipped cream on top of each slice, of cake and lay the chocolate curls on top of the whipped cream. **3.** Spoon a pool of warm, White Chocolate Sauce on one side of the cake and a pool of warm, Dark Chocolate Sauce on the other side and serve immediately.

ROSEMARY CRÈME BRÛLÉE

This is a classic recipe for crème brûlée (which simply means "burnt cream" in French) with a fresh twist. The custard is infused with fresh rosemary, which adds another dimension of subtle flavor and helps offset the richness of the dessert. Dried rosemary is not a happy substitute for fresh in this situation as it lacks the fragrant oils needed to perfume the custard. The crème brûlée may be made a day in advance and kept refrigerated, but the caramel crust should be added just before serving.

Every chef has a different theory on how to best apply the caramelized sugar crust. We simply sprinkle the cooled custards with sugar and melt the sugar with a blow torch. It affords much more control than a broiler and is easier to do than pouring liquid caramelized sugar on top of the custard.

MAKES SIX 5-OUNCE CUSTARDS

1. Preheat the oven to 300 degrees. **2.** In a 2-quart saucepan set over medium heat, combine the cream, milk, and rosemary. Bring just to a boil and remove from the heat. **3.** Place the egg yolks in a large bowl and whisk in the confectioners' sugar. Beat until the yolks are pale yellow and slightly thickened. **4.** Slowly whisk the hot cream mixture into the yolk mixture. Strain through a fine sieve into a 2-quart pitcher and skim off any foam. **5.** Place six 5-ounce ceramic or glass crème brûlée molds in a baking pan with 2-inch sides. Pour the custard mixture into the molds. Using a paper towel, blot any bubbles floating on top. **6.** Place the baking pan in the oven and pour hot water around the custards until it reaches halfway up the sides of the molds. Cover the pan with aluminum foil and bake the custards for 30 minutes, or until the tip of a paring knife inserted into the center of the custards comes out just barely sticky. Do not overcook. **7.** Carefully remove the pan from the oven, take the custards out of the water bath, and cool to room temperature. Refrigerate the custards for several hours.

TO SERVE: 1. Sprinkle each custard evenly with about 1 tablespoon granulated sugar. Wipe any excess sugar off the rims of the molds. **2.** Hold a lit blowtorch with a medium flame about 6 inches from the top of each custard and move the flame evenly over the surface, allowing the sugar to melt and caramelize. Make sure all the sugar has melted. Let cool for several minutes to let the sugar harden. **3.** Serve garnished with a sprig of fresh rosemary.

CUSTARDS
3 cups heavy cream
¾ cup milk
5-inch sprig fresh rosemary, stems removed
10 egg yolks
¾ cup sifted confectioners' sugar

CARAMELIZED CRUST
6 tablespoons granulated sugar

GARNISH
6 small sprigs fresh rosemary

GINGER SCONES

We serve these heart-shaped scones to arriving guests with jasmine tea. They're best served slightly warm with clotted cream and strawberry jam. The scones can be frozen or stored for several days in an airtight container.

2½ cups all-purpose flour
5 teaspoons baking powder
5 tablespoons sugar
3 tablespoons cold butter, diced
½ cup milk
½ cup heavy cream
1 egg yolk
½ cup minced candied ginger

MAKES 20 SCONES

1. Preheat the oven to 375 degrees. 2. Line two baking sheets with waxed paper. 3. In the bowl of an electric mixer or food processor, combine the flour, baking powder, sugar, and butter. Add the milk, ¼ cup of the cream, the egg yolk, and the candied ginger and continue mixing just until the ingredients are incorporated. (Overmixing will cause the scones to be tough.) 4. Turn the dough out onto a lightly floured board and roll out to a thickness of ¾ inch. Stamp the dough out using a small heart-shaped cookie cutter or a 2-inch round cutter and place the scones on the baking sheets. Brush the tops with the remaining cream. 5. Bake for 4 minutes, rotate, and bake for 5 minutes more. Remove from the sheets with a spatula and cool on a wire rack.

Basic Pie Dough (see page 157; croissant
dough or puff pastry may be substituted)

8 thick stalks red rhubarb

1 quart water

1½ cups sugar

1 cup Raspberry Puree (see page 138)

Nonstick cooking spray

¼ cup sugar combined with 1 teaspoon
ground cinnamon

Ginger Ice Cream (see page 150)

My Grandmother's Rhubarb Pizza with Ginger Ice Cream

Although my grandmother really did have a rhubarb patch, she wasn't into making pizzas. But if she had been, they probably would have tasted something like these. (A chef has to take a little poetic license once in a while to keep his clients intrigued.)

In the restaurant, we use a flaky croissant dough for the crust, but any pie dough will work. The pizzas may be completely assembled well in advance and baked just before serving.

MAKES SIX INDIVIDUAL 5-INCH ROUND PIZZAS

1. On a floured board, roll the dough out to about ⅛ inch thick. Lay a bowl about 5 inches in diameter upside down on the dough and, using the rim as a pattern, cut out six circles with a sharp paring knife. Place the pastry rounds between sheets of waxed paper and refrigerate. 2. Wash the rhubarb, trim off any leaves, and cut out any brown or bruised spots. Using a very sharp knife, slice six of the stalks on the bias about ⅛ inch thick. Roughly chop the remaining two stalks and keep separate. 3. In a 4-quart saucepan, combine the water, sugar, and Raspberry Puree over medium heat. Bring just to a boil. 4. Place the rhubarb slices in a stainless steel bowl and carefully pour the hot liquid over them just to cover, leaving about 2 cups liquid in the saucepan. 5. Add the chopped rhubarb to the liquid left in the pan and simmer until very soft. Remove from the heat. Strain the rhubarb, reserving the liquid, and puree in a food processor or blender until smooth. 6. Return the liquid to the stove and simmer until reduced to a syrupy consistency.

TO ASSEMBLE PIZZAS: 1. Preheat the oven to 375 degrees. 2. Remove the pastry rounds from the refrigerator. Spray several baking sheets with nonstick cooking spray and lay the pastry rounds on them. Spread about 1 tablespoon of the rhubarb puree evenly over each round. Lift the rhubarb slices out of their liquid and arrange on top of the puree in a single layer of concentric circles. 3. Bake pizzas in the lower half of the oven for 6 to 8 minutes, or until the pastry is crisp and golden brown. Remove from the oven and brush each pizza with the reduced rhubarb syrup.

TO SERVE: 1. Sprinkle each of six serving plates lightly with cinnamon sugar in a ribbonlike pattern. 2. Place a warm, glazed pizza on each plate and top with a small scoop of Ginger Ice Cream.

10 ounces finest-quality imported white chocolate, broken into small pieces

½ cup sugar

¼ cup water

4 egg whites

2 tablespoons dark rum

1 tablespoon vanilla extract

1¼ cups heavy cream

WHITE CHOCOLATE MOUSSE

Most chocolate mousses are made with either whipped cream or egg whites. This luxurious version combines an Italian meringue made with egg whites for body as well as whipped cream for airiness. A little dark rum adds a depth charge of rich flavor. The same recipe can be used to make a dark chocolate mousse. Just substitute semisweet dark chocolate for the white chocolate.

It's fun to serve the dark and white mousses together in little oval egg shapes or decoratively piped from a pastry bag. We often serve this with a sharp citrus sauce, such as passion fruit, to offset the sweetness of the chocolate.

SERVES 4 TO 6

1. Melt the chocolate in a large stainless steel bowl set over a pot of simmering water. 2. In a 1-quart saucepan, combine the sugar and water and bring to a boil. Allow the liquid to boil until it reaches the soft-ball stage—234 to 240 degrees on a candy thermometer. 3. Meanwhile, in the bowl of an electric mixer, begin beating the egg whites until they begin to form soft peaks. Slowly pour the hot sugar syrup into the egg whites in a thin stream, whisking constantly. Whip until the bottom of the bowl is no longer hot. Then pour the melted chocolate onto the meringue mixture and blend thoroughly, scraping down the sides of the bowl with a rubber spatula. 4. Add the rum and vanilla and continue beating until all the ingredients are incorporated. 5. In a separate bowl, whip the cream just until it begins to form stiff peaks. Using a rubber spatula, gently fold the whipped cream into the chocolate mixture in three batches until the cream is evenly distributed. 6. Pour the mousse into a chilled container and refrigerate until set.

TO SERVE: Put the mousse into a pastry bag fitted with a decorative tip and pipe into goblets or serving dishes or use an oval ice cream scoop dipped in warm water to scoop the mousse out onto chilled serving plates.

3 pints fresh raspberries

1 tablespoon fresh lemon juice

3 to 4 tablespoons sugar

RASPBERRY PUREE

MAKES 1 CUP

1. Puree the berries in a food processor. Strain through a fine strainer to remove all the seeds, pressing hard on the solids with a rubber spatula to extract all the liquid. 2. Add the lemon juice and mix well. 3. Add the sugar 1 tablespoon at a time, tasting after each addition, until the desired sweetness is obtained.

NOTE: You may substitute frozen raspberries, but reduce the sugar by one-half.

BERNARD LOISEAU'S CHOCOLATE MOUSSE CAKE

In celebration of the fortieth anniversary of the founding of Relais & Chateaux, an organization of the world's finest hotels and restaurants in forty nations, Bernard Loiseau, a three-star Michelin chef from Saulieu, France, came to America for the first time to cook a dinner with me at The Inn at Little Washington Bernard's restaurant and hotel, La Côte d'Or, is in a little village in the Burgundian countryside about two hours from Paris. He has become very well known for his innovative use of the products of that region.

Although we had a lot in common, Bernard couldn't speak English, and I don't speak French. Fortunately, his lovely wife, Dominique, was fluent in English and stood between us at the stove until we got our bearings. We all ended up having a wonderful time working together and became good friends. This is one of the desserts Bernard presented for the occasion — a dense, incredibly unsweet, chilled chocolate mousse cake with a meringue center. The meringue should be made a day in advance.

SERVES 8

TO MAKE THE MERINGUE: **1.** Preheat the oven to 150 degrees. Line a baking sheet with parchment. **2.** In the bowl of an electric mixer fitted with a whisk attachment, whisk the egg whites until they form soft peaks. Slowly add the confectioners' sugar and continue whisking until doubled in volume. **3.** Place the meringue in a pastry bag fitted with a plain tip. On the baking sheet, working from the center outward, pipe a continuous coil of meringue to a diameter of 7 inches. **4.** Bake for 10 hours, until crisp and dry.

TO MAKE THE MOUSSE: **1.** Line an 8-inch round cake pan with parchment paper. **2.** Melt the chocolate in a stainless steel bowl set over a pot of simmering water. Remove from the heat and whisk in the egg yolks one at a time. Set the mixture aside and keep warm. **3.** In the bowl of an electric mixer fitted with a paddle attachment, whip the butter and slowly add the cocoa powder until thoroughly incorporated. Add the chocolate and egg yolk mixture and mix well. Set aside. **4.** In a clean bowl of an electric mixer fitted with a whisk attachment, whip the egg whites until they form soft peaks. With a rubber spatula, gently fold the egg whites into the chocolate mixture in thirds. **5.** Place the mousse in a pastry bag fitted with a plain tip and pipe the mixture into the cake pan. Fill the pan half full. Lay the meringue disc on top and gently press into place. Pipe the remaining chocolate mixture into the pan, allowing it to fill in around the sides of the meringue. **6.** Chill for 2 hours.

TO SERVE: Run a warm paring knife around the inside rim of the pan to loosen the cake and invert it onto a serving tray. Carefully remove the parchment paper and dust with unsweetened cocoa powder.

6 perfectly ripe peaches
2 teaspoons lemon juice
Granulated sugar to taste (optional)
1 cup heavy cream
1½ tablespoons confectioners' sugar
Peach Ice Cream (recipe follows)
1 quart Vanilla Ice Cream
(see page 154)
Peach Sorbet (recipe follows)
6 tablespoons peach schnapps
or peach liqueur

GARNISH

6 sprigs fresh mint

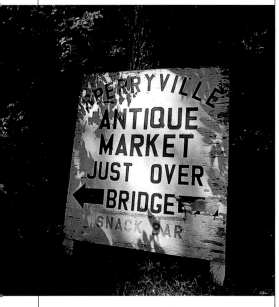

6 egg yolks
2 cups sugar
1 quart peach puree (about 3 pounds of
fresh peaches, peeled, stoned, and pureed)
Pinch of salt
1 quart heavy cream
1 tablespoon vanilla extract
2 cups fresh peaches, peeled, stoned, and
coarsely chopped

8 very ripe fresh peaches, peeled, stoned,
and pureed in a blender or food processor
Simple Syrup (see page 166)
¼ cup peach schnapps or peach liqueur
(optional)

THE PEACH INTENSIFIER

The next time you find yourself with a bushel of ripe peaches that you have no idea what to do with, try this intriguing sundae. It's nicknamed "Peaches Five Ways" and is composed of a scoop each of peach and vanilla ice cream, peach sorbet, sliced peaches, and peach puree—all spritzed with peach schnapps. If you don't have time to make the ice cream or the sorbet, cheat a little and purchase good-quality commercial brands and serve sliced fresh peaches and peach puree with them.

SERVES 6

1. In a large pot, bring 2 quarts of water to a simmer. Score the bottoms of the peaches and, using a wire strainer, submerge the peaches in the hot water for about 5 to 10 seconds to loosen the skins. Immediately plunge the peaches into a bowl of ice water. Remove and peel. **2.** Remove the stone from three of the peaches and puree with the lemon juice in a blender or food processor. If desired, add a little sugar to the puree. Chill in the refrigerator until ready to use. **3.** Remove the stone from the remaining three peaches and cut into small wedges. Place in a bowl and cover with cold water. Refrigerate until ready to serve. **4.** In the bowl of an electric mixer, whip the cream with the confectioners' sugar until stiff. Place in a pastry bag fitted with a decorative tip and refrigerate.

TO SERVE: In each of six fancy ice cream dishes, place one scoop of the peach and vanilla ice creams and one scoop of the sorbet. Top with peach slices and peach puree and sprinkle with 1 tablespoon of the schnapps or liqueur. Pipe rosettes of sweetened whipped cream on top and garnish with a mint sprig.

PEACH ICE CREAM

MAKES 1 GALLON

1. In the top of a double boiler or in a stainless steel bowl set over a pan of simmering water, whisk the egg yolks and sugar together until warm to the touch. Add the peach puree and salt. Whisking constantly, continue cooking until the custard thickens slightly. **2.** Remove from the heat and add the cream, vanilla, and chopped peaches. Chill in the refrigerator, then freeze in an ice cream machine according to the manufacturer's instructions.

PEACH SORBET

MAKES 1 QUART

1. In a medium-size bowl, combine the peach puree and an equal amount of Simple Syrup. Add the schnapps or liqueur (if using) and strain. **2.** Freeze in an ice cream machine according to the manufacturer's instructions.

2 quarts Simple Syrup (see page 166)
1 cup fresh lemon juice
¼ cup Campari
Pinch of salt
2 tablespoons finely
chopped fresh rosemary
1 egg white, beaten until
medium peaks form

LEMON-ROSEMARY SORBET
WITH CAMPARI

*The flavors in this unusual sorbet stimulate the appetite. For this reason,
it is most often served at The Inn to cleanse the palate between courses. Be sure
to chop the rosemary just before you're ready to use it, as it will turn black if
it is chopped too far in advance.*

MAKES 2½ QUARTS

1. In a medium-size bowl, combine the Simple Syrup, lemon juice, Campari, salt, and rosemary. **2.** Transfer to an ice cream machine. When the mixture becomes slushy, add the egg white. Freeze in an ice cream machine according to the manufacturer's instructions.

1½ cups Simple Syrup (see page 166)
⅔ cup fresh grapefruit juice
1 teaspoon dried tarragon
¼ teaspoon lightly chopped fresh
tarragon
2 tablespoons Campari
Pinch of salt

GRAPEFRUIT-TARRAGON SORBET

*This sorbet makes a perfect between-course palate cleanser or a refreshing
dessert when combined with fresh grapefruit sections.*

MAKES 1 PINT

1. In a 1-quart saucepan, combine the Simple Syrup, grapefruit juice, and dried tarragon over medium heat. Bring to a boil and remove from the heat. Cool for 15 minutes. **2.** Strain the sauce, discarding the dried tarragon. Add the fresh tarragon, Campari, and salt. Freeze in an ice cream machine according to the manufacturer's instructions.

1 quart apple cider, preferably
unpasteurized
1 cup Riesling
1 cup sugar
5 cinnamon sticks
1 teaspoon whole cloves
1 teaspoon whole allspice

MULLED CIDER SORBET

MAKES 1 QUART

1. In a medium-size nonreactive saucepan, combine the cider, Riesling, sugar, cinnamon sticks, cloves, and allspice. Simmer until reduced to 1 quart. Strain. **2.** Chill in the refrigerator, then freeze in an ice cream machine according to the manufacturer's instructions.

HONEYDEW SORBET

1½ cups honeydew puree

3 cups Simple Syrup (see page 166)

¼ cup Midori (optional)

PASSION FRUIT SORBET

1½ cups passion fruit puree or frozen orange juice concentrate

3 cups Simple Syrup (see page 166)

WATERMELON SORBET

1½ cups watermelon puree

3 cups Simple Syrup (see page 166)

1 tablespoon fresh lemon juice

1 tablespoon grenadine

½ cup dried black currants soaked overnight in ½ cup Midori

1 cup Raspberry Puree (see page 138)

1 cup Crème Anglaise (see page 157)

4 ounces semisweet chocolate, melted

A WATERMELON FANTASY

If you have a little time on your hands and guests who will appreciate your efforts, this is a stunning summertime showstopper. It's also incredibly refreshing. We often serve it as a "preliminary" dessert as part of a tasting menu.

Watermelon sorbet is layered in a bowl with honeydew and passion fruit purees forming the "rind" with "seeds" made from currants soaked in melon liqueur. It is then unmolded, sliced, and presented on a white plate decorated to look like a red-and-white checked picnic table cloth complete with faux chocolate covered ants.

Fortunately, it can be made a day or two in advance.

SERVES 8

1. Chill a 3-quart stainless steel bowl in the freezer for at least 20 minutes. **2.** To make the honeydew sorbet, combine the honeydew puree, Simple Syrup, and Midori (if using) in an ice cream machine. **3.** Spread the honeydew sorbet ½ inch thick over the entire interior of the chilled bowl. Return the bowl to the freezer. **4.** To make the passion fruit sorbet, combine the passion fruit puree or orange juice concentrate and Simple Syrup in the ice cream machine. **5.** Spread the passion fruit sorbet ⅛ to ¼ inch thick over the honeydew sorbet. Return the bowl to the freezer. **6.** To make the watermelon sorbet, combine the watermelon puree, Simple Syrup, lemon juice, and grenadine in the ice cream machine. Stir in the Midori-soaked currants. **7.** Spoon the watermelon sorbet into the bowl and return to the freezer for 3 hours.

TO SERVE: 1. Place the Raspberry Puree, Crème Anglaise, and melted chocolate in squirt bottles. **2.** Chill eight serving plates in the freezer for 20 minutes. **3.** Remove the plates from the freezer and draw stripes of Raspberry Puree and Crème Anglaise across the plates in a checkerboard pattern. Make chocolate "ants" by placing three contiguous droplets of chocolate on the plates and, using a toothpick, dragging the droplets out in the shape of an ant's legs and antennae. **4.** Remove the bowl of sorbets from the freezer and invert it onto a cutting board. Gently lift off the bowl. Using a sharp knife dipped in hot water, slice the sorbet into wedges. **5.** Place a wedge of the Watermelon Fantasy in the center of each decorated plate. (To keep the wedges from slipping, you may wish to put a pinch of sugar in the center of the plate.)

2½ cups half-and-half
1¼ cups sugar
½ cup peeled and finely chopped
fresh ginger
½ teaspoon lemon juice
3 egg yolks
2 tablespoons minced candied ginger

6 eggs
1½ cups firmly packed brown sugar
¼ cup confectioners' sugar
4 teaspoons ground cinnamon
1½ teaspoons ground allspice
1½ teaspoons ground nutmeg
½ teaspoon ground ginger
1 teaspoon ground cloves
½ teaspoon salt
2 cups milk
2½ cups pumpkin puree
1 quart heavy cream
4 teaspoons vanilla extract

GINGER ICE CREAM

This is one of our favorite ice creams. The unexpected tingling heat of fresh ginger in combination with the frozen ice cream creates an exciting confusion for the brain and palate. In the winter we serve this along with Earl Grey tea and lemon ice cream in a little Chinese bowl with warm plum "soup." It is luscious.

MAKES 1 QUART

1. In a medium saucepan, combine the half-and-half, ½ cup of the sugar, and the fresh ginger. Bring to a boil, then reduce to a simmer and cook for 5 minutes. **2.** Remove from the heat and allow to steep for 10 minutes more. Stir in the lemon juice. **3.** In a large stainless steel bowl, whisk the egg yolks and the remaining ¾ cup sugar until thick and foamy. Slowly pour the half-and-half mixture into the yolk mixture, whisking vigorously until thoroughly incorporated. **4.** Set the bowl over a pot of simmering water and cook, whisking constantly, until the mixture coats the back of a spoon. **5.** Remove from the heat and strain. Cool in the refrigerator, then freeze in an ice cream machine according to the manufacturer's instructions. When the ice cream begins to stiffen, add the candied ginger and continue to churn until the ginger is evenly incorporated and the ice cream is thick.

PUMPKIN ICE CREAM

MAKES 2 QUARTS

1. In the top of a double boiler or in a stainless steel bowl set over a pan of simmering water, whisk together the eggs, brown sugar, confectioners' sugar, cinnamon, allspice, nutmeg, ginger, cloves, and salt. Cook until the mixture thickens slightly and coats the back of a spoon. Remove from the heat. **2.** Meanwhile, in a 2-quart saucepan, scald the milk. **3.** Slowly add the hot milk to the egg mixture. Whisk in the pumpkin, cream, and vanilla. **4.** Strain the custard through a fine sieve. Chill in the refrigerator, then freeze in an ice cream machine according to the manufacturer's instructions.

¾ cup (1½ sticks) lightly salted butter

¼ pound pecan halves

1 cup milk

2½ cups heavy cream

1 cup sugar

9 egg yolks

Caramel Sauce (see page 128)

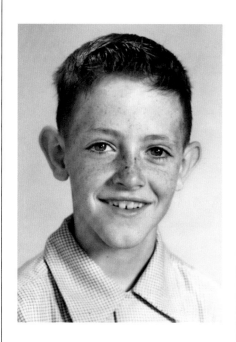

5 egg yolks

1⅓ cups sugar

2 cups milk

2 cups heavy cream

½ vanilla bean, split lengthwise

1¼ cups buttermilk

BUTTER PECAN ICE CREAM

As a kid, I never believed that store-bought butter pecan ice cream really contained any butter, and the little chunks didn't really taste like pecans. I liked to think about the way it might have tasted in a perfect world. This recipe is a child's fantasy of how real *butter pecan ice cream ought to taste.*

MAKES 8 TO 10 SERVINGS

1. In a large skillet, melt the butter over medium heat. Add the pecans and sauté until the butter begins to turn golden brown. 2. Remove the skillet from the heat and strain the butter into a stainless steel container and reserve. Cool to room temperature. Reserve the pecans in a separate container. 3. In a 2-quart heavy-bottomed saucepan, combine the milk, cream, and ½ cup of the sugar. Heat until just scalded. Do not boil. Remove from the heat and set aside. 4. In a large stainless steel bowl, whisk together the egg yolks and the remaining ½ cup sugar until well blended. 5. Place the bowl over boiling water (or use a double boiler) and, whisking constantly, heat until hot to the touch, about 110 degrees. 6. Slowly add the scalded milk mixture to the yolk mixture, whisking constantly. After thoroughly mixing, strain through a mesh strainer into the reserved butter and whisk together. 7. Chill in the refrigerator, then freeze in an ice cream machine according to the manufacturer's instructions. When the ice cream begins to stiffen, sprinkle in the reserved pecans and continue to churn until the nuts are evenly incorporated and the ice cream is thick.

TO SERVE: Serve the ice cream in individual dishes topped with Caramel Sauce.

BUTTERMILK ICE CREAM

The old-fashioned taste of this ice cream is wonderful in a shortcake or as a simple accompaniment to fresh blueberries.

MAKES ABOUT 2 QUARTS

1. In the top of a double boiler set over medium heat, whisk together the egg yolks and sugar until slightly thickened and foamy. 2. In a medium-size saucepan, combine the milk and cream. Add the vanilla bean and scald. 3. Slowly pour the hot milk mixture into the egg mixture, whisking constantly, and continue to cook over medium heat until the custard coats the back of a spoon. Remove from the heat and strain. 4. Cool to room temperature and add the buttermilk. Freeze in an ice cream machine according to the manufacturer's instructions.

ROASTED BANANA ICE CREAM

Roasting the bananas in their skins for 10 to 15 minutes is the secret to this rich, intensely banana-flavored ice cream. We serve it as an unusual accompaniment to a chocolate soufflé and they go bananas.

MAKES 1 QUART

1. Preheat the oven to 350 degrees. **2.** Lightly oil the bananas and place them on a baking sheet. Bake for 10 to 15 minutes, or until they are dark and soft. **3.** Remove the bananas from the oven and peel. Puree in a food processor and set aside. **4.** In a large stainless steel bowl, whisk together the egg yolks and sugar until light and foamy. **5.** In a large saucepan set over medium heat, combine the milk and cream. Bring to a boil. **6.** Remove from the heat and slowly pour into the yolk mixture, whisking rapidly. Add the banana puree and rum. **7.** Strain and cool. Freeze in an ice cream machine according to the manufacturer's instructions.

CARAMEL ICE CREAM

This rich and luscious ice cream makes an excellent accompaniment to nut tarts or cakes. The flavor is haunting and intense, so a little goes a long way. Caramel lovers can combine it with old-fashioned Vanilla Ice Cream (see page 154) and Caramel Sauce (see page 128) for a sophisticated sundae.

MAKES 1½ PINTS

TO MAKE THE CARAMEL: **1.** In a 2-quart heavy-bottomed saucepan, scald the cream and keep warm. **2.** In a 4-quart saucepan, combine the sugar and water over medium heat. Stir until the sugar dissolves and the liquid is clear. Increase the heat to high and cook, without stirring, until the liquid begins to turn a golden amber color. **3.** Immediately remove from the heat and slowly add the scalded cream. (Caution: When the cream hits the hot sugar, it will steam up and spatter, so be sure to pour the cream slowly, averting your face and protecting your hands.) Stir the mixture until smooth, then whisk in the butter. Let cool.

TO MAKE THE ICE CREAM: **1.** In a 2-quart heavy-bottomed saucepan, scald the cream and milk. **2.** In a stainless steel bowl set over a pan of simmering water or in the top of a double boiler, quickly whisk together the egg yolks and sugar. **3.** Add the scalded milk and cream to the yolk mixture and whisk over medium-high heat until thick enough to coat the back of a spoon. Remove from the heat. **4.** Add the caramel. Chill in the refrigerator, then freeze in an ice cream machine according to the manufacturer's instructions.

2 tablespoons vegetable oil
(approximately)
4 ripe bananas, unpeeled
6 egg yolks
1½ cups sugar
2 cups milk
2 cups heavy cream
2 tablespoons dark rum

CARAMEL
1¼ cups heavy cream
1½ cups sugar
½ cup water
½ cup (1 stick) unsalted butter

ICE CREAM
2 cups heavy cream
1 cup milk
6 egg yolks
1⅓ cups sugar

2 quarts heavy cream
1 quart milk
2 vanilla beans
12 egg yolks
2⅔ cups sugar

VANILLA ICE CREAM

MAKES ABOUT 1 GALLON

1. In a large, heavy-bottomed saucepan, combine 1 quart of the cream and the milk.
2. Split the vanilla beans in half lengthwise. Using a paring knife, scrape out the seeds. Add the seeds and pods to the milk and cream and bring just to a boil. Set aside.   **3.** In the top of a large double boiler or in a stainless steel bowl set over a pot of boiling water, whisk together the egg yolks and sugar. Slowly pour in the scalded milk and cream, whisking constantly. Cook until thick enough to coat the back of a spoon.   **4.** Remove from the heat. Lift out the vanilla beans. Add the remaining 1 quart cream. Chill in the refrigerator, then freeze in an ice cream machine according to the manufacturer's instructions.

9 ounces finest-quality imported white chocolate, broken into small pieces
3 egg yolks
⅔ cup sugar
2 cups milk
¼ cup dark rum
1 tablespoon vanilla extract
1 cup heavy cream
Dark Chocolate Sauce (recipe follows)

WHITE CHOCOLATE ICE CREAM

White Chocolate Ice Cream with warm Dark Chocolate Sauce has been a favorite of our guests for years. This really is the ultimate chocolate sundae.

The simple secret for making it taste extraordinary is to use a very fine-quality imported chocolate. Best to offer small portions, as no one can stop eating it once it's set in front of them.

MAKES 1 QUART

1. Melt the chocolate in a stainless steel bowl set over a pan of simmering water.
2. In the top of a double boiler set over medium heat, whisk together the egg yolks and sugar. Cook until slightly thickened and foamy.   **3.** Meanwhile, in another saucepan, scald the milk.   **4.** Slowly pour the hot milk into the yolk mixture and, whisking constantly, cook over medium heat until the custard coats the back of a spoon. Add the melted chocolate. Strain and cool.   **5.** Add the rum, vanilla, and cream. Freeze in an ice cream machine according to the manufacturer's instructions.

TO SERVE: Serve with Dark Chocolate Sauce.

8 ounces good-quality semisweet chocolate, broken into small pieces
¼ cup strong coffee
3 tablespoons Grand Marnier
3 tablespoons heavy cream

DARK CHOCOLATE SAUCE

MAKES 1½ CUPS

1. Place the chocolate in a double boiler or stainless steel bowl set over a pot of simmering water. Add the coffee, Grand Marnier, and cream. Heat, whisking occasionally, until the chocolate melts and the mixture is smooth.   **2.** Hold the sauce over warm water until you're ready to serve it. Or refrigerate and gently rewarm it before serving.

8 ounces finest-quality imported
white chocolate, coarsely chopped

3 tablespoons heavy cream

3 tablespoons triple sec

WHITE CHOCOLATE SAUCE

MAKES 1¼ CUPS

1. In the top of a double boiler, combine the chocolate, cream, and triple sec. Heat, stirring occasionally, over barely simmering water until the chocolate is melted. **2.** This sauce may be kept in a squirt bottle in the refrigerator and submerged in hot water for a few minutes prior to using.

CHOCOLATE BOURBON-PECAN TART

1½ cups sugar

⅓ cup water

1 cup heavy cream

1 cup pecans

¼ cup bourbon

¼ cup (½ stick) butter, melted

1 whole egg

1 egg yolk

1 prebaked tart or pie shell
(9 or 10 inches in diameter)

4 ounces bittersweet chocolate, melted

This chewy confection tastes like the Deep South. It keeps beautifully for three to four days in the refrigerator and can be cut into very thin wedges to serve with tea or offered as a dessert along with a little bourbon-laced whipped cream. We always feature it on our buffet table during our Christmas Open House for the town citizens—a group of bourbon aficionados.

SERVES 8

1. In a small, heavy-bottomed saucepan, bring the sugar and water to a boil over medium heat. Cook until golden brown. **2.** Quickly remove the pan from the heat and slowly and carefully pour the cream into the caramelized sugar. (*Caution:* When the cream hits the hot sugar, it will steam up and spatter, so be sure to avert your face and protect your hands.) **3.** Cook the caramel-cream mixture over low heat for 3 minutes, stirring to dissolve any lumps of caramel. **4.** Preheat the oven to 350 degrees. **5.** Strain the mixture through a sieve and allow it to cool for 15 minutes. **6.** Place the pecans on a baking sheet and toast in the oven for 5 to 7 minutes, or until lightly browned. Remove and set aside. Increase the oven temperature to 400 degrees. **7.** Whisk the bourbon, butter, egg, and yolk into the cooled caramel mixture. Stir in the toasted pecans. **8.** Brush the tart or pie shell with the melted chocolate and pour the filling into the shell. Bake in the center of the oven for 15 minutes. Reduce the heat to 350 degrees and continue baking for an additional 15 minutes.

TO SERVE: Serve the tart at room temperature.

CRÈME ANGLAISE

This is our version of basic English custard sauce, which can be flavored in a variety of ways to complement a specific dessert. Very fresh brown eggs are the secret to achieving the desired rich taste and bright golden color. Fine-quality vanilla beans (the best are from Tahiti) are also important and well worth the cost. The vanilla beans can be stored in a tightly sealed container of sugar, and they will infuse the sugar with their flavor. The vanilla sugar can then be used in cookies, ice creams, etc.

MAKES 2½ CUPS

1. Using a sharp paring knife, split the vanilla bean in half lengthwise. 2. In a 2-quart saucepan over medium heat, combine the half-and-half and split vanilla bean. Bring just to a boil. Remove from the heat and set aside. 3. Remove the vanilla bean halves and scrape the seeds out of the pods. Return the seeds and pods to the liquid. 4. Meanwhile, in a medium-size stainless steel bowl, whisk together the egg yolks, sugar, and lemon zest until the mixture is pale yellow and doubled in volume. 5. Beginning with a few drops at a time, whisk the scalded half-and-half into the egg mixture. After about ¼ cup of the hot liquid has been incorporated, whisk in the rest more rapidly. 6. Pour the custard back into the saucepan and cook over medium heat, stirring constantly with a wooden spoon, until the custard thickens (170 degrees on a candy thermometer). Do not let boil. 7. Remove the custard from the heat and strain through a fine sieve. Refrigerate for up to several days before serving.

TO SERVE: Serve the sauce very cold.

1 whole vanilla bean
2 cups half-and-half
4 egg yolks
¼ cup sugar
½ teaspoon grated lemon zest

BASIC PIE DOUGH

ONE 9- TO 10-INCH CRUST

1. Sift the flour into a medium-size bowl. Add the butter and shortening or oil and cut into small pieces with a pastry cutter or two knives. Work the mixture with your fingertips until it resembles coarse cornmeal. 2. Make a well in the center of the mixture and add the water, kneading until the dough forms a ball. 3. Wrap the dough tightly in plastic wrap and refrigerate for at least 30 minutes. 4. When you're ready to use the dough, roll it out on a lightly floured surface and proceed with your recipe.

2 cups all-purpose flour
⅓ cup butter
⅓ cup shortening or vegetable oil
⅓ cup ice water

1 white grapefruit
2 cups sugar

CANDIED GRAPEFRUIT RIND

This is the secret recipe of our neighbor, Mattie Ball Fletcher, now 106 years old, who used to make the candied rind for us until she was about 98, at which time she passed it on to a young mountain woman in our kitchen.

We used to take Mother Ball, as she is referred to locally, all the rinds left over from squeezing grapefruit juice at breakfast, and she would candy them for us. They were then offered with chocolates and petite fours to our guests after dinner. Soon the rinds became famous and much written about. According to Mother Ball, it's not really a secret at all, "just right much work."

MAKES APPROXIMATELY 28 PIECES

1. Cut the grapefruit into four wedges and, using a tablespoon, scoop the fruit away from the rinds. (Save fruit for another use.) **2.** Place the rinds in a medium-size saucepan and cover with water. Lay a weight or heavy plate on top of the rinds to keep them submerged. Bring the water to a boil and continue boiling for 20 minutes. **3.** Strain the rinds. Add fresh water to the pot, weight the rinds, and boil for another 20 minutes. **4.** Strain the rinds again. Add 1 cup of the sugar and cover with fresh water. Weight the rinds and boil for another 20 minutes, or until rinds are translucent and sticky. **5.** Strain the rinds for a third time. Place on a metal rack and set aside in a warm, dry place for at least 24 hours. **6.** When the rinds are relatively dry, slice lengthwise into ⅛-inch strips and toss in the remaining 1 cup sugar. The rinds may be stored at room temperature in the sugar for up to about 10 days.

8

STOCKS, SAUCES, AND SUNDRY

1 package (1 tablespoon) dry yeast

1 tablespoon sugar

1 tablespoon salt

7½ tablespoons caraway seeds

2½ cups rye flour

3 cups bread flour

2 cups warm (95 degrees) water

1 cup coarsely chopped pecans

1 cup dried black currants or raisins

Nonstick cooking spray

¼ cup kosher salt

SALT-CRUSTED CURRANT RYE BREAD

We've been serving this bread for years, and our guests continue to rave about it. It's surprisingly easy to make and freezes beautifully. Form it into long, slender loaves and slice it very thinly with a serrated knife as a cocktail bread. You'll find it to be the perfect accompaniment to cheese or smoked salmon.

MAKES 3 LOAVES

1. In the 5-quart bowl of an electric mixer fitted with a dough hook, combine the yeast, sugar, salt, 1½ tablespoons of the caraway seeds, the rye flour, and bread flour. Mix until thoroughly combined.   2. With the mixer running, slowly add the water and mix until the dough forms a ball and leaves the sides of the bowl. This will take about 2 minutes.   3. Add the pecans and currants or raisins and mix for 2 minutes more.   4. Turn the dough out onto a floured board. Wipe out the mixing bowl and spray nonstick cooking spray. Return the dough to the bowl, cover with a damp tea towel, and place in a warm (about 85 degrees) spot for about 1 hour, or until the dough has doubled in size.   5. Punch the dough down to release the trapped gases. Form it into 3 loaves approximately 12 inches long and 2 inches wide. Brush with cold water and sprinkle generously with the kosher salt and remaining 6 tablespoons caraway seeds.   6. Place the loaves on a lightly greased baking sheet and let sit in a warm place for about 20 minutes. Meanwhile, preheat the oven to 350 degrees.   7. Bake for 30 minutes, turning the pan every 10 minutes or so to ensure even browning.   8. Cool on a wire rack.

5 cups rolled oats

1½ cups raw, unsalted whole cashews or cashew pieces

1½ cups shredded unsweetened coconut

1 cup wheat germ

1 cup soy flour

1 cup sesame seeds

1 cup slivered almonds

1 cup safflower or other vegetable oil (not olive oil)

1 cup honey

Nonstick cooking spray

GRANOLA

Long before we opened the restaurant, we ate this granola every morning, always joking that it was the reason we were still alive. Nowadays, we serve it at The Inn for breakfast. It's delicious, healthful, and wonderfully easy to make. It also happens to be the favorite treat of our dogs, Rose and DeSoto. They'll do anything for a nugget of it. We always pack it for a snack on long trips. You can find all of the ingredients at your neighborhood health-food store.

MAKES 3 QUARTS

1. Preheat the oven to 325 degrees   **2.** In a large bowl, combine the oats, cashews, coconut, wheat germ, soy flour, sesame seeds, and almonds, stirring well with a wooden spoon.   **3.** Add the oil and stir well.   **4.** Add the honey and stir to combine.   **5.** Spray several large baking sheets with nonstick cooking spray and spread the granola evenly, about 1 inch deep, on the sheets.   **6.** Bake, turning frequently, for about 25 minutes, or until golden brown. (If you prefer your granola in smaller pieces, it can be easily broken up while still warm.)   **7.** Let cool to room temperature and store in a large tin or plastic bags. The granola will keep very well for several weeks or longer unrefrigerated.

4 tablespoons butter

½ teaspoon cayenne pepper

2 teaspoons Cajun seasoning

2 teaspoons ground cumin

3 tablespoons sugar

1 pound pecans

SPICY PECANS

We serve these pecans slightly warm with cocktails. Our guests find them addictive and so will your friends. They also make a perfect host or hostess gift. The pecans can be used in our barbecued lamb recipe (see page 86) and are great in a cornbread stuffing for turkey.

MAKES 4 CUPS

1. In a large skillet over medium-high heat, melt the butter until it begins to foam.   **2.** Add the cayenne, Cajun seasoning, cumin, and sugar. Mix well, then add the pecans. Cook for about 3 minutes, stirring or tossing constantly, until the pecans are well toasted and lightly colored.   **3.** Pour the pecans onto a wire rack placed over a baking sheet. Let cool to room temperature.   **4.** Store in an airtight container until ready to serve. Warm before serving.

9 cups water

4 cups sugar

Simple Syrup

MAKES 2 QUARTS

1. Combine the water and sugar in a heavy-bottomed saucepan over medium heat. Stir until the sugar is completely dissolved and the liquid is clear. Remove from the heat and cool to room temperature.   2. Store indefinitely in the refrigerator.

2 tablespoons minced shallot or onion

1 dried ancho pepper, softened in warm water for 15 minutes, stemmed, and minced

1 jalapeño pepper, seeded and minced

2 cups good-quality lingonberry preserves (available in most specialty food stores)

1 tablespoon fresh lime juice

Pinch of cayenne pepper

1 tablespoon minced fresh cilantro

Lingonberry Salsa

This is a delightfully simple condiment that can be put together in minutes. It transforms a simple roast pork dinner into something very special and is the perfect accompaniment for venison. It keeps for weeks well sealed in the refrigerator and makes a lovely Christmas gift.

At Thanksgiving, we make this salsa with cranberries and serve it with turkey. Our guests find it much more interesting than the typical cranberry relish.

MAKES 2½ CUPS

1. In a medium-size bowl, combine all the ingredients, stirring with a wooden spoon until well blended.   2. Store in the refrigerator until ready to use. Allow the salsa to come to room temperature before serving.

1 teaspoon dry mustard

2 tablespoons minced fresh tarragon or 1½ teaspoons dried

¼ teaspoon minced garlic

½ teaspoon chopped shallot

1 teaspoon salt

1 tablespoon fresh lemon juice

2 teaspoons raspberry vinegar

⅓ cup red wine vinegar, preferably imported

1 cup extra-virgin olive oil

Freshly ground pepper to taste

Tarragon Vinaigrette

MAKES 2 CUPS

1. Whisk all the ingredients together in a large stainless steel bowl. Transfer to a jar with a tight-fitting lid.   2. Store in the refrigerator and shake well or whisk thoroughly before using.

MUSTARD MAYONNAISE

MAKES ¼ CUP

1 tablespoon Dijon mustard
¼ cup mayonnaise, preferably homemade
½ tablespoon dry mustard
Salt and freshly ground pepper to taste

1. Whisk together the Dijon mustard, mayonnaise, dry mustard, and salt and pepper in a small bowl or blend in a food processor. 2. Store in the refrigerator until ready to use.

GREEN HERB MAYONNAISE

This sauce takes just minutes to make in a food processor and transforms a simple grilled fish into a memorable meal. Nothing is better with cold salmon. You can vary the herbs depending on what is available in the market or your garden.

MAKES 2 CUPS

2 teaspoons capers, drained
¼ cup tightly packed fresh dill, stems removed
¼ cup tightly packed fresh Italian parsley, stems removed
¼ cup tightly packed watercress, stems removed
2 tablespoons fresh tarragon leaves
1 cup mayonnaise, preferably homemade
1 tablespoon Dijon mustard
2 teaspoons fresh lemon juice
½ teaspoon salt
Freshly ground pepper to taste

1. Place the capers, dill, parsley, watercress, and tarragon in a food processor fitted with a steel blade and pulse until coarsely chopped. Scrape down the sides of the bowl with a rubber spatula and pulse again. 2. Add the mayonnaise, mustard, lemon juice, salt, and pepper and blend thoroughly. 3. Store in the refrigerator until ready to use.

1 tablespoon rice wine vinegar
7 tablespoons nuoc mam
2 tablespoons sugar
½ cup cold water
Juice of 1 lime
2 tablespoons finely julienned carrot
¼ cup minced fresh cilantro
2 large cloves garlic, peeled and minced
2 jalapeño peppers, ribs and seeds
removed, finely chopped

CLEAR FISH SAUCE WITH
LIME AND CILANTRO

I love Vietnamese food—particularly the little spring rolls wrapped in rice paper accompanied by a fragrant dipping sauce. The elusive flavors in that dipping concoction are the inspiration for this easy-to-make sauce. The secret ingredient is a bit of inexpensive, fermented fish sauce called nuoc mam, *which is available in oriental markets.*

We always keep clear fish sauce on hand in the refrigerator to use as a light dressing for oriental-style salads or to serve as a healthful sauce replacement with fish, pork, or chicken. It's perfect for someone on a low-fat diet because it's virtually fat free but explosively flavorful.

MAKES 1 CUP

1. Mix all the ingredients together in a medium-size bowl, stirring until the sugar is dissolved.   **2.** Store in the refrigerator until ready to use.

HERB BUTTER

Back in the days when fresh herbs were still a novelty in American kitchens, we used to serve this simple herb butter to show off our herb garden. The guests are still requesting it.

Herb butter is great to keep on hand in the refrigerator to add quick pizzazz to grilled fish, steak, or even baked potatoes. It's fabulous for basting roasted chicken or spreading on tea sandwiches. You may wish to develop your own favorite combination of herbs using this recipe as a guideline.

MAKES 1 CUP

1 cup (2 sticks) butter, softened
1 teaspoon minced fresh Italian parsley
1 teaspoon minced green onion
½ teaspoon minced watercress
1 teaspoon minced fresh tarragon

1. In the bowl of an electric mixer fitted with a paddle attachment, mix the butter, parsley, green onion, watercress, and tarragon on low speed until the herbs are evenly distributed throughout.   **2.** Place the butter in a crock for serving. Or roll it into a sausage shape, wrap in plastic wrap, and refrigerate. When firm, slice into ½-inch disks.   **3.** Store in the refrigerator.

CHARDONNAY BUTTER SAUCE

There will always be certain dishes that absolutely scream out for a little butter sauce to achieve that essential sensuousness. If you're concerned about fat (and who isn't?), don't just say no—say less. A tiny pool of this butter sauce, which the French call beurre blanc, will suffice.

Any white wine and any white wine vinegar may be used, but we find that chardonnay and champagne vinegar give the sauce a unique character. It is important to use a mixture of salted and unsalted butter to achieve the ideal taste.

MAKES 1¼ CUPS

½ cup chardonnay
½ cup champagne vinegar
1 shallot, peeled and sliced in half
½ cup (1 stick) cold lightly salted butter, cut into tablespoon-size pieces
½ cup (1 stick) cold unsalted butter, cut into tablespoon-size pieces
Salt and white pepper to taste
Fresh lemon juice (optional)

1. In a small saucepan over high heat, combine the chardonnay, vinegar, and shallot. Boil until reduced to about 3 tablespoons and almost syrupy.   2. Reduce the heat to low and, piece by piece, stir in the salted and unsalted butter with a wooden spoon, incorporating one piece of butter before adding the next. Continue until all the butter is used up.   3. Remove the shallot from the sauce. Add the salt and white pepper and several drops of lemon juice (if using). Keep the sauce warm (not hot) until ready to serve.

NOTE: It used to be thought that this sauce could not be held for any length of time, but fortunately that myth has been debunked. It keeps nicely in a stainless steel canister resting in a water bath at 125 degrees for several hours. Some clever home cooks hold it in a thermos bottle on the back of the stove. Be aware that if it becomes too cold or too hot, it may separate and look like plain old melted butter instead of the satiny sauce it's meant to be. If you find yourself the victim of this misfortune, here's a little trick for bringing the sauce "back": Simply bring 3 tablespoons of heavy cream to a boil in a small saucepan and reduce for a few minutes until syrupy. Remove from the heat and gradually whisk the "broken" sauce into the cream and it will regain its lustrous consistency.

BROWN BUTTER

MAKES 1 CUP

½ pound lightly salted butter

In a heavy skillet over medium heat, melt the butter, stirring constantly. Increase the heat and continue stirring as the butter foams and begins to turn golden brown. Immediately remove the butter from the heat and carefully pour it into a heat-proof container.

*4 pounds chicken bones
(backs and necks)*

1½ cups coarsely chopped carrot

1 cup coarsely chopped celery

1 cup chopped onion

1 sprig fresh rosemary

1 sprig fresh thyme

1 bay leaf, crumbled

1 tablespoon whole black peppercorns

Salt to taste

CHICKEN STOCK

MAKES 2 QUARTS

1. Place the bones in a large stockpot over high heat and cover with cold water. When the stock comes to a simmer, skim off any foam or residue that rises to the surface. **2.** Add the carrot, celery, onion, rosemary, thyme, bay leaf, and peppercorns. Simmer for 2 to 3 hours. **3.** Strain the stock and season with salt. Let cool to room temperature and refrigerate. **4.** Remove the fat from the surface of the cold stock before using.

NOTE: The flavor of the finished stock can be intensified by bringing it to a boil and reducing it over high heat. Chicken stock may be frozen or kept for up to a week in the refrigerator if it is brought to a boil every three days.

¼ cup peanut oil

10 pounds veal bones

3 onions, coarsely chopped

3 carrots, coarsely chopped

3 stalks celery, coarsely chopped

2 cups dry white wine

2 cloves garlic

3 medium-size tomatoes, cored

3 sprigs fresh parsley

2 bay leaves, crumbled

¼ teaspoon dried thyme

2 tablespoons whole black peppercorns

*½ pound mushroom stems and pieces
(optional)*

Salt to taste

VEAL STOCK

MAKES 3 QUARTS

1. Preheat the oven to 450 degrees. **2.** Place the peanut oil in a large roasting pan and add the bones, onion, carrot, and celery. Place the pan in the oven and reduce the heat to 350 degrees. When the bones and vegetables are a rich brown color, place them in a large stockpot. **3.** Scrape all the flavorful drippings from the roasting pan into the pot. Pour 1 cup of hot water into the pan, set it over high heat, and boil for a minute or so to release any of the flavorful bits remaining. Add the water to the stockpot. **4.** Add the wine and enough cold water to the pot to cover the bones by 1 inch. Bring the stock to a gentle boil, skimming off any foam that rises to the surface. Lower the heat, add the garlic, tomatoes, parsley, bay leaves, thyme, peppercorns, and mushrooms (if using). Simmer for 3 to 4 hours. **5.** Strain the stock and season with salt. Let cool to room temperature and refrigerate. **6.** Remove the fat from the surface of the cold stock before using.

Sources

D'Artagnan
399-419 St. Paul Street
Jersey City, NJ 07306
Tel: (800) 327-8246
Fax: (201) 792-6113
Fresh foie gras, game, poultry, and home-made pâtés

Browne Trading Corp.
Rod Mitchell
260 Commercial Street
Portland, ME 04101
Tel: (207) 766-2402
Fax: (207) 766-2404
Scallops in the shell

Sweet Water Aqua
P.O. Box 298
Edgewater, NJ 07020
Tel: (800) 477-2967
Fax: (201) 224-5688
Freshwater blue prawns

Gourmand
66 South Pickett Street
Alexandria, VA 22304
Tel: (703) 461-0600
Fax: (703) 461-0198
Gourmet specialty foods

Bernardaud North America
41 Madison Avenue
New York, NY 10010
Tel: (212) 696-2433
Fine porcelain Limoges

Valrhona Chocolat
1901 Avenue of the Stars
Suite 1774
Los Angeles, CA 90067
Tel: (310) 277-0401
Fax: (310) 277-4092
Fine French chocolate

Summerfield Farm
10044 James Monroe Hwy.
Culpeper, VA 22701
Tel: (540) 547-9600
Fax: (540) 547-9628
Rabbit and venison

Calhoun's Ham House
211 S. East Street
Culpeper, VA 22701
Tel: (540) 825-8319
Virginia country ham

INDEX

ABOUT THE AUTHOR

A native of Washington, D.C., PATRICK O'CONNELL began his restaurant career at the age of fifteen, quite by accident, working in a neighborhood restaurant after school.

As a student of speech and drama at Catholic University of America, he financed his education working as a waiter. After a year spent traveling in Europe, he began to find the "living theater" of the restaurant business more compelling than a career as an actor.

He found the mountains of Virginia a good antidote to the pressures of the restaurant world, and, in 1972, together with his partner, Reinhardt Lynch, he began a catering enterprise in the Shenandoah Valley that ultimately evolved into The Inn at Little Washington.

The Inn is a member of the Paris-based Relais & Chateaux Association, and it became the first establishment in America to achieve two five-star awards in the same year from the Mobil Travel Guide, five diamonds from the American Automobile Association, and the top national rating in the Zagat Hotel Survey, with the first "perfect" score for its cuisine in the history of the Zagat rating system. The James Beard Awards named Patrick O'Connell "Best Chef—Mid-Atlantic" and chose The Inn at Little Washington as Restaurant of the Year in 1993.

Patrick O'Connell was one of the original inductees into "Who's Who of Food and Beverage in America." He lives in Washington, Virginia.

ABOUT THE TYPE

This book was set in Cochin, named for Charles Nicolas Cochin the younger, an eighteenth-century French engraver. Mr. Henry Johnson first arranged for the cutting of the Cochin type in America, to be used in *Harper's Bazaar.*

Cochin type is a commendable effort to reproduce the work of the French copperplate engravers of the eighteenth century. Cochin is a versatile and attractive face.